A Baptist at the Crossroads

Monographs in Baptist History

VOLUME 20

SERIES EDITOR
Michael A. G. Haykin, The Southern Baptist Theological Seminary

EDITORIAL BOARD
Matthew Barrett, Midwestern Baptist Theological Seminary
Peter Beck, Charleston Southern University
Anthony L. Chute, California Baptist University
Jason G. Duesing, Midwest Baptist Theological Seminary
Nathan A. Finn, North Greenville University
Crawford Gribben, Queen's University, Belfast
Gordon L. Heath, McMaster Divinity College
Barry Howson, Heritage Theological Seminary
Jason K. Lee, Cedarville University
Thomas J. Nettles, The Southern Baptist Theological Seminary, retired
James A. Patterson, Union University
James M. Renihan, Institute of Reformed Baptist Studies
Jeffrey P. Straub, Independent Scholar
Brian R. Talbot, Broughty Ferry Baptist Church, Scotland
Malcolm B. Yarnell III, Southwestern Baptist Theological Seminary

Ours is a day in which not only the gaze of western culture but also increasingly that of Evangelicals is riveted to the present. The past seems to be nowhere in view and hence it is disparagingly dismissed as being of little value for our rapidly changing world. Such historical amnesia is fatal for any culture, but particularly so for Christian communities whose identity is profoundly bound up with their history. The goal of this new series of monographs, Studies in Baptist History, seeks to provide one of these Christian communities, that of evangelical Baptists, with reasons and resources for remembering the past. The editors are deeply convinced that Baptist history contains rich resources of theological reflection, praxis and spirituality that can help Baptists, as well as other Christians, live more Christianly in the present. The monographs in this series will therefore aim at illuminating various aspects of the Baptist tradition and in the process provide Baptists with a usable past.

A Baptist at the Crossroads

The Atonement in the Writings
of Richard Furman (1755–1825)

Obbie Tyler Todd

Foreword by Tom J. Nettles

⌖PICKWICK *Publications* · Eugene, Oregon

A BAPTIST AT THE CROSSROADS
The Atonement in the Writings of Richard Furman (1755–1825)

Monographs in Baptist History 20

Copyright © 2021 Obbie Tyler Todd. All rights reserved. Except for brief quotations in critical publications or reviews, no part of this book may be reproduced in any manner without prior written permission from the publisher. Write: Permissions, Wipf and Stock Publishers, 199 W. 8th Ave., Suite 3, Eugene, OR 97401.

Pickwick Publications
An Imprint of Wipf and Stock Publishers
199 W. 8th Ave., Suite 3
Eugene, OR 97401

www.wipfandstock.com

PAPERBACK ISBN: 978-1-7252-9703-6
HARDCOVER ISBN: 978-1-7252-9704-3
EBOOK ISBN: 978-1-7252-9705-0

Cataloguing-in-Publication data:

Names: Todd, Obbie Tyler, author. | Nettles, Tom J., foreword

Title: A Baptist at the crossroads : the atonement in the writings of Richard Furman (1755–1825) / by Obbie Tyler Todd; foreword by Tom J. Nettles.

Description: Eugene, OR: Pickwick Publications, 2021 | Series: Monographs in Baptist History | Includes bibliographical references and index.

Identifiers: ISBN 978-1-7252-9703-6 (paperback) | ISBN 978-1-7252-9704-3 (hardcover) | ISBN 978-1-7252-9705-0 (ebook)

Subjects: LCSH: Furman, Richard, 1755–1825. | Atonement. | Baptists—Doctrines. | Baptists—History.

Classification: BX6495.F85 T63 2021 (paperback) | BX6495.F85 (ebook)

08/23/21

Contents

Foreword by Tom J. Nettles | vii

Acknowledgments | xi

    1. Introduction | 1

    2. Furman's Moderate Calvinism | 8

    3. Furman's Two-Part Doctrine of Atonement | 38

    4. A Systematic Theological Treatment of Furman's Doctrine of Atonement | 63

    5. Critical Analysis of Furman's Doctrine of Atonement | 89

Bibliography | 105

Name/Subject Index | 111

Scripture Index | 113

Foreword

GET READY FOR AN adventure in cultural history and historical theology. Obbie Todd argues that "Richard Furman held to both a penal substitutionary theory of the atonement as well as to a moral governmental view." This has been stated clearly throughout and argued from a variety of documents. It includes insight into why moral government ideas seemed to adhere to many of the southern theologians as they absorbed them into their views of honor.

He illustrates Furman's clear perceptions of the meaning of these two theological views and Furman's familiarity with the leading thinkers and documents that set forth the leading features of each. The author observes that Furman "integrated these two models by downplaying the commercial nature of the atonement." Except on rare and non-public occasions, Furman avoided the language of payment in its many forms. I personally detect a bit more commercialism in the language of Furman than the author has admitted, but I concede that in this matter, due to the importance and centrality of the issue, that silence and careful circumlocutions indicate that Furman wanted to have room for embracing discreet elements of the moral government theory. Todd has made his point well on this issue. The integration of these two apparently antagonistic viewpoints was achieved largely through "emphasizing forgiveness as a divine pardon instead of a debt paid, and describing faith as the application of Christ's work." Furman did indeed give some kind of autonomy to the idea of pardon that made it rise above a certain and necessary connection with a debt paid. Also, the existential point of faith as the actual transfer of the sinner from condemnation to justification, from alienation to reconciliation, and from enmity to adoption as sons helps illustrate the amalgamation. How faith related to Christ's obedience, death, and intercession was captured beautifully in the quote from Furman that faith "consists in a firm persuasion, on the testimony of heaven, that Jesus is the Son of God, and the only Savior of men; and in such a reliance on his justifying righteousness, atoning blood, and living intercession, as causes us to cleave to him as the anchor of our hope, the ark of our safety, and city of our refuge."

The author has investigated thoroughly the Furman corpus, both published and unpublished, has gone to the relevant archives and has become saturated in the language of Furman. This has armed him with an ability to expand doctrinal ideas from Furman's verbal shorthand and rhetoric inferring accurately the larger "Furmanian" doctrine behind the sermonic flourishes. The book benefits greatly from that acute familiarity and uncovers an excellent grasp of the entire system of doctrine from which Furman developed his sermonic emphases and his circular letters, and that fueled his rhetorical fires. One also will be informed by Todd's grasp of the relevant secondary sources both on Furman and on the development of moral government theology. These sources have been produced by well-seasoned, trustworthy, source-rich historians and their summaries provide just the kind of guidance one needs in developing general principles from a highly complex and deeply diverse movement. The author has used these sources well and has added his own analysis of many of the primary sources behind them.

This narrative invites a discussion of the apparent dualities in the areas of satisfaction, justice, and substitution on the one hand and forgiveness, grace, and mercy on the other. This is especially pertinent in the discussions of "Legal vs. Commercial" and "Pardon vs. Payment." The implication throughout advanced moral government doctrine is that if sufficient payment is made for an offense, then the forgiveness or pardon ensuing is not really of grace, and not applied by sovereign mercy, but is granted as a right. If forgiveness is merited, is it really of grace? It seems, according to the narrative, that this was the tension known by Furman as he sought to negotiate some synthesis of penal, propitiatory, substitution with the leading strengths of moral government. This book communicates well this noble attempt of Furman. Todd's succinct summary of the merger is stated in his coining of the concept "governmental substitution." Readers will want to contemplate the viability of seeking to blend two systems of thought that have fundamental contradictions at their core. Can a system that rejects imputation and one that depends on imputation ever be reconciled or synthesized without fundamentally altering definitive elements of one or both systems? Given that noble attempt by Furman, the term appears to be an excellent summary of what Furman proposed to do. The historical display of Furman's hybrid could provoke healthy discussion of the highest order.

In summary, the thought, theology, and pastoral style of Richard Furman come alive in this excellent work by Obbie Todd. In this fine synthesis of primary and secondary source work, Todd has successfully presented Furman as an "eclectic theologian." Early influences from both the Separate Baptists and the Regular Baptists conditioned Furman to seek the biblical aspect of different ways of thinking without surrendering the final authority of Scripture. In particular, Todd carefully crafts Furman's understanding of the elements of truth in the moral government theory without sacrificing the doctrines of propitiation and substitution emphasized in the Charleston Association Confession of Faith. Todd shows that Furman operated under the assumption that these treatments were not "mutually exclusive," but could be "partially blended" with some nuancing of the strict peculiarities of each. Todd's treatment is an admirable model of historical theology as well as a careful engagement with intellectual history.

> Tom J. Nettles
> Senior Professor, Historical Theology
> The Southern Baptist Theological Seminary

Acknowledgments

I would like to thank my wife, Kelly, for all her love and support during the process of researching and writing this book. Also, my church family has been a source of encouragement and strength. Dr. Adam Harwood, my doctoral supervisor, has proven to be an advisor, counselor, and guide as I composed this work. I also owe many thanks to Dr. Tom Nettles for introducing me to the life and thought of Richard Furman and for sparking an interest in Baptist history. Ultimately, every word and every chapter of this book were by God's grace.

1

Introduction

South Carolina Baptist Richard Furman (1755–1825) personified a host of seeming contradictions. As the inaugural president of the first Baptist denomination in America and pastor of First Baptist Church of Charleston, Furman was a leader among Regular Baptists and an architect for the South Carolina Baptist Association. Yet his own backcountry conversion in the High Hills of Santee came by the preaching of Separate Baptist Joseph Reese, the man who eventually ordained Furman.[1] Thomas J. Nettles has described Furman as "a Southern embodiment of the best of Puritanism" for his piety, his confessionalism, and his sense of social order.[2] However, oddly enough, Furman was also an ardent patriot whose support for the American Revolution was so vehement that British General Cornwallis offered a bounty for Furman, "so notorious [a] rebel."[3] Furman was an educated Baptist, an almost oxymoronic label in the eighteenth century. Alvin Reynolds explained, "He was fortunate to have had enlightened, well-to-do parents, while the majority of the Baptists of his day came from homes of the poor and unlearned."[4] In the same state that later produced the likes of John C. Calhoun and Andrew Jackson, and among the same Baptists who championed Thomas Jefferson as a political hero, Furman was in fact a Federalist.[5] Though a stalwart for religious liberty, Furman also campaigned

---

1. Rogers, *Richard Furman*, 18. Reese was censured by the Sandy Creek Association for his cooperation with Regular Baptists. Kidd, *Great Awakening*, 363–64.
2. Nettles, "Richard Furman," 140.
3. For the details of this account, see Rogers, *Richard Furman*, 39.
4. Reynolds, "The Life and Work of Richard Furman," 115.
5. Hatch, *Democratization of American Christianity*, 95.

for the right of ministers to serve in the South Carolina state legislature.[6] Tragically, Furman did not see the contradiction between extolling the moral government of God and defending the practice of slavery, a position he articulated in detail.[7] The life and thought of Richard Furman represent the confluence of theological, social, and political forces, many of which appear incongruent.

Richard Furman's doctrine of atonement exhibited this same complexity. Furman was a Calvinistic Baptist in the mold of the Charleston Confession of Faith (1767); however, to label Furman a "Calvinist" does not describe adequately his view of the atonement.[8] Furman labored to show that biblical fidelity included more than a Procrustean adherence to Calvinism. His doctrine of atonement was not monolithic but included different themes and tropes. He upheld both rectoral and retributive justice in Christ's atoning work while soft-pedaling commutative justice in order to accentuate distributive justice.[9] Contrary to later Calvinistic Baptists such as James P. Boyce, Furman did not believe penal substitutionary and moral governmental views of the atonement were mutually exclusive.[10] Unlike his protégé William B. Johnson, Furman did not believe a moral governmental view of the atonement precluded the concept of imputation. In many ways,

---

6. Baker and Craven, *Adventure in Faith*, 206.

7. See Furman, *Exposition of the Views of the Baptists Relative to the Coloured Population of the United States in Communication to the Governor of South Carolina*.

8. Oliver Hart, Furman's predecessor at FBC Charleston, helped produce *The Charleston Confession* and *Summary of Church Discipline*.

9. Rectoral justice denotes the kind of justice that vindicates God as ruler or governor. Louis Berkhof explained, "This justice, as the very name implies, is the rectitude which God manifests as the Ruler of both the good and the evil. In virtue of it He has instituted a moral government in the world, and imposed a just law upon man, with promises of reward for the obedient, and threats of punishment for the transgressor" (Berkhof, *Systematic Theology*, 75). Retributive justice, on the other hand, is the type of justice that dispenses reward or punishment for its own sake or based on what is deserved. Berkhof defined retributive justice as that "which relates to the infliction of penalties. It is an expression of the divine wrath" (Berkhof, *Systematic Theology*, 75). Commutative justice refers to that which is owed between individuals, including business transactions or an exchange of goods. Distributive justice, on the other hand, concerns the fair allocation of goods in a society.

10. Penal substitution is a theory of the atonement that holds that Christ died on the cross as a substitute in the place of sinners in order to receive their penalty for sin. Simon Gathercole made a helpful distinction: "One can have substitution without that being *penal* substitution, that is, without *punishment* for sins involved. These are often treated together: what is taken *in our stead* is the penalty for sins" (Gathercole, *Defending Substitution*, 18–19). In contrast, moral government is a theory of the atonement that holds that, by Jesus Christ's death on the cross, God demonstrated his divine displeasure for sin and vindicated himself as a righteous lawgiver.

Furman stood at the intersection of confessional Calvinism and Edwardsean Calvinism, even when many believed the two were at odds.[11] In this sense, Richard Furman's doctrine of atonement mirrored that of Andrew Fuller. Likewise, Furman's insistence that faith applied the work of Christ influenced his belief in the sufficiency of Christ's atonement to save all as well as its efficiency to save only some.[12] While remaining theologically consistent with historic Calvinism, Furman believed that Scripture demanded a more robust picture of the atoning work of Christ.

In this monograph, I will contend that Richard Furman held to both a penal substitutionary theory of the atonement as well as to a moral governmental view. He integrated these two models by downplaying the commercial nature of the atonement, emphasizing forgiveness as a divine pardon instead of a debt paid, and describing faith as the application of Christ's work.

The methodology of this monograph is twofold, elucidation and contextualization. Through an analysis of Furman's writings, his doctrine of

---

11. In some sense, to juxtapose confessional and Edwardsean Calvinism is a false dichotomy. Though a Congregationalist, Jonathan Edwards instructed his children in the Westminster Shorter Catechism and confessed to Scottish Presbyterian John Erskine, "As to my subscribing to the substance of the Westminster Confession, there would be no difficulty" (Edwards, *Works of Jonathan Edwards, Volume 16*, 355). Jonathan Edwards did not so much depart from confessional Calvinism as he renovated Reformed doctrines with newer concepts. For instance, within the doctrine of total depravity he developed the distinction between natural and moral ability. His view of irresistible grace included a strong emphasis upon the religious affections. In his view of divine providence, Edwards articulated a compatibilist notion of the freedom of the will. Edwards also blended a moral governmental view of the atonement with a penal substitutionary model. Edwards Amasa Park, a devoted follower of Edwards's disciple Samuel Hopkins and Abbot Professor of Theology at Andover Theological Seminary, described Edwardsean Calvinism in these words: "It signifies the formal creed which a majority of the most eminent theologians in New England have explicitly or implicitly sanctioned, during and since the time of [Jonathan] Edwards [Senior]. It denotes the spirit and genius of the system openly avowed or logically involved in their writings. It includes not the peculiarities in which Edwards differed, as he is known to have differed, from the larger part of his most eminent followers, nor the peculiarities in which any one of his followers differed, as some of them did, from the larger part of the others; but it comprehends the principles, with their logical sequences, which the great number of our most celebrated divines have approved expressly or by implication" (Park, "New England Theology," 169–217). In this book, the epithet "Edwardsean" will denote any of these "principles" that found their origin in the thought of Jonathan Edwards or that were shared by a number of Edwards's disciples, such as Joseph Bellamy and Samuel Hopkins. Richard Furman imbibed these "principles" through Andrew Fuller and Timothy Dwight, both of whom affiliated with Bellamy and Hopkins.

12. In his critique of the Edwardsean combination of rectoral and retributive justice, S. Mark Hamilton defined the "rectoral demands" of justice as those that seek to "restore honor" to the Moral Lawgiver ("Re-Thinking Atonement in Jonathan Edwards and New England Theology," 85–99).

the atonement will be distilled and explicated. The special collections office in the Duke Library at Furman University in Greenville, South Carolina, offered a generous amount of Furman's personal correspondence, his sermons, and his public tracts. Most of these are not included in G. William Foster Jr.'s *Life and Works of Dr. Richard Furman, D.D.*[13] They reveal more fully Furman's Calvinism and his interest in the progress of Calvinism in both the North and the South.

A key for interpreting Furman's theology will be his moderate form of Calvinism. Furman was known for his disdain for "systems," and he praised those fellow Baptists who shared his aversion.[14] Furman discussed the doctrines of total depravity and unconditional election frequently, yet the doctrine of limited atonement is mentioned rarely in any of his writings, suggesting that Furman was indeed a "moderate" Calvinist as Wiley Richards has labeled him.[15] This moderation is a helpful framework by which to understand Richard Furman. Furman's doctrine of atonement was consistent with most Calvinists of his day, but not dogmatically so. Furman seems to blend ideas that are seemingly incompatible, such as moral governmental and penal substitutionary models, and limited and unlimited atonement. Furman believed that all were found in Scripture.

By interacting with the work of Oliver Crisp in his treatment of "non-penal substitution" and "penal non-substitution" models, Furman can be distinguished from other Edwardsean thinkers and even Jonathan Edwards himself. The work of Simon Gathercole will aid in categorizing Furman's view of substitution. Comparisons with theologians like James P. Boyce and William B. Johnson will reveal the unique aspects of Furman's doctrine of atonement in relation to other Calvinistic Baptists.

Furman's doctrine of atonement will be contextualized in terms of his social, political, and theological milieu. According to Nettles, "The two major influences, therefore, on Furman's doctrinal stance were the Charleston Association's theological documents, decidedly Calvinistic in content, and

---

13. Foster, *Life and Works of Dr. Richard Furman, D.D.*

14. According to W. T. Brantly, Furman "thought that many of the advocates of exact system in Theology had not deserved well of the cause, and that it accorded better with Christian wisdom to adopt an unmutilated Revelation, than to press it by forced constructions into the service of a system." Brantly, "Extracts from Dr. W. T. Brantly's Sermon Delivered in 1825," 221. Furman described his best friend, Edmund Botsford, in this way: "He was, in a word, what has been called a moderate Calvinist: yet his sentiments were not formed by any human system, but by what he considered the true meaning of the word of God" (Furman, "Sketch of the Life of the Rev. Edmund Botsford, A.M.," 462.

15. Richards, *Winds of Doctrines*, 18.

the Whitefieldian conversionism of the First Great Awakening."[16] Furman's view of the atonement reveals both of these doctrinal influences. From southern culture to the American Revolution, external factors will be explored in order to apprehend better Furman's thought.

Although Richard Furman never authored a systematic theology or penned a treatise on the atonement, the absence of these works in no way implies that his doctrine of atonement is indecipherable. While Furman's extant writings are mainly in the form of sermons and circular letters, these documents are saturated with soteriological thinking. When William B. Johnson thought back to the preaching of his mentor, he recounted,

> I remember hearing him, more than forty years ago, preach from the text, "I am set for the defense of the Gospel"—it was truly a masterful effort. Never shall I forget his solemn, impressive countenance, his dignified manner, his clear statements of the Gospel doctrine and precepts, his unanswerable arguments in support of the Gospel's claim to a Divine origin, the lofty sentiments that he poured forth, the immovable firmness with which he maintained his position, and the commanding eloquence with which he enforced the whole argument.[17]

Such was the preaching of Richard Furman: precise, relentlessly logical, and evangelical to the core. Richard Furman's entire theological system inhered in his doctrine of the atonement. As a revivalist, pastor, and Christian leader, Furman was virtually incapable of speaking on any issue without recourse to the gospel. At the epicenter of the Furmanian gospel was the atonement. His numerous thoughts on the "atoning blood, meritorious righteousness and prevailing intercession of the gracious Immanuel" are sufficient to indicate his positions on the nature, extent, and intent of the atonement.[18] In this book, I will focus primarily on the nature of the atonement while drawing out Furman's views on the extent and intent of the atonement as well.

Furman is a monumental figure in Baptist history. G. William Foster Jr. has concluded that Furman is "America's most influential Baptist."[19] His doctrine of atonement warrants further examination. This monograph is an attempt to provide theological clarity to a Baptist figure who has not received the due appreciation and study his ministry deserves. In this study,

---

16. Nettles, "Richard Furman," 146.

17. Johnson, "Richard Furman, D.D.," 13–14.

18. Furman, "On the Analogy between the Dispensations of Grace by the Gospel, and a Royal Marriage Feast," 468.

19. Foster, "Preface," xviii.

I will seek to delineate Richard Furman's theory of the atonement and how he achieved such a view.

Currently, no study on Richard Furman's doctrine of the atonement exists. A sum total of two sentences were dedicated to Furman's doctrine of the atonement in David Allen's tome *The Extent of the Atonement: A Historical and Critical Review*.[20] In the second edition of *Baptist Theologians* published in 2000, the chapter on Richard Furman was omitted in an effort to condense and concentrate on more notable Baptist figures.[21] In 1962, Alvin Reynolds wrote a basic dissertation on the life and work of Furman; however, no investigation was made into Furman's theology.[22] Interestingly, James Leo Garrett's acclaimed *Baptist Theology: A Four-Century Study* does not even mention Furman.[23] Further still, Furman's views of the nature of the atonement and the moral governmental motif in his soteriology have not been investigated in any significant sense. Tom Nettles has provided perhaps the most substantive look into Furman's theology in his chapter on Furman in *Baptist Theologians*.[24] In the second volume of *The Baptists*, Nettles also devotes a chapter to Furman, providing some overlapping material.[25] Nevertheless, Nettles neither explicates Furman's doctrine of atonement nor investigates the influences that shaped Furman's theology. Relative to his impact in American Baptist history, few depictions of Richard Furman are extant. James A. Rogers's *Richard Furman: Life and Legacy* (2001) remains the only modern biography of any substance.[26] Therefore it comes as little surprise that there exists no study on Richard Furman's doctrine of the atonement, a doctrine that held particular importance for the way Furman preached the gospel. For such a critical figure in Baptist history, Furman's doctrine of atonement warrants further examination.

A study of Richard Furman's doctrine of the atonement will shed light on one of the most influential Baptist figures in American religious history. Furman's doctrine of atonement will provide greater clarity into the debate over Regular and Separate Baptist theologies and perhaps demonstrate that these schools were not so opposed as has been assumed. This study will demonstrate how Baptist theologians and leaders were shaped theologically by the political and social circumstances of their generation. As an ardent

---

20. Allen, *Extent of the Atonement*, 500, 651, 653.
21. George and Dockery, *Baptist Theologians*.
22. Reynolds, "Richard Furman."
23. Garrett, *Baptist Theology*.
24. Nettles, "Richard Furman."
25. Nettles, "Richard Furman (1755–1825)," 125–52.
26. Rogers, *Richard Furman: Life and Legacy*.

supporter of the American Revolution and someone who shared a close friendship with the likes of Patrick Henry, Richard Furman was a man of his era. He adopted constitutional, governmental, and even kingly language to describe the atonement. These influences will be examined in detail. In this book, I will demonstrate also how the theme of "honor" imbued the theology and ethics of late eighteenth century Baptists and how it shaped their views on the atonement.

2

Furman's Moderate Calvinism

Systems and Sectarianism

AT FIRST GLANCE, W. Wiley Richards's description of the confessionalist Richard Furman as a "moderate" Calvinist seems a bit left of the mark.[1] After all, Furman once hailed his good friend Oliver Hart as a "fixed Calvinist."[2] According to Foster, "Furman's words regarding his predecessor at Charleston, Oliver Hart, were self-defining."[3] However, in the same breath he also commemorated Hart as a "consistent, liberal Baptist" for his mentor's friendly, ecumenical spirit. Like Hart, the substance of Furman's faith was Calvinistic, but the ethos of his faith was considerably less rigid. Wiley's description of Furman is fitting because Furman never allowed any human scheme or sect to come before the authority of the Bible. Ironically, during the course of his fifty-one-year ministry, the man who led the first national Baptist denomination in America and subscribed faithfully to the *Charleston Confession* eschewed two things more than most: systems and sectarianism. This flexible quality imbued every aspect of Furman's theology.

The system-averse Furman often warned that obedience to Holy Scripture required more than a Procrustean adherence to confessional Calvinism. The preacher from High Hills "thought that many of the advocates of exact system in Theology had not deserved well of the cause, and that it accorded better with Christian wisdom to adopt an unmutilated Revelation, than to

---

1. Richards, *Winds of Doctrines*, 18.
2. Furman, "Rewards of Grace Conferred on Christ's Faithful People," 337.
3. Foster, "Preface," xiii.

press it by forced constructions into the service of a system."[4] In this sense, Furman was indeed a "moderate" Calvinist, unrelenting in the essentials of Calvinism yet unwilling to allow any human framework to have the final say. In his funeral sermon for Edmund Botsford, Furman characterized his best friend and protégé much as he might have described himself: "He was, in a word, what has been called a moderate Calvinist: yet his sentiments were not formed by any human system, but by what he considered the true meaning of the word of God."[5] Furman was first and foremost a biblicist. He believed that a commitment to the authority of Scripture necessarily implied some resistance to human-made systems.

Likewise, while Furman saw the value of a Baptist denomination, he was by no means a denominationalist. His anti-sectarianism was an extension of his suspicion of systems. In his mind, Baptists should not be so wedded to their own way of thinking as to isolate themselves from non-Baptist theologians. For instance, in his eulogy of John Gano, Furman celebrated Gano's aversion to dogmatic Calvinism:

> The doctrines he embraced were those which are contained in the Baptist Confession of Faith, and are commonly styled Calvinistick. But he was of a liberal mind, and esteemed pious men of every denomination. While he maintained with consistent firmness, the doctrines which he believed to be the truths of God, he was modest in the judgment which he formed of his own opinion, and careful to avoid giving offense, or grieving any good man, who differed from him in sentiment.[6]

Furman revered Gano so much that he eventually named two of his sons John Gano (the first dying in infancy). Furman's Baptist eulogies indicate that he esteemed those Baptists who prized "consistent firmness" of Calvinist doctrines but without the kind of hostile sectarianism he felt posed a danger to Baptists in the South. Furman was indeed an ecumenical Baptist, and he was remembered as such. In his eulogy of Furman, W. T. Brantly encapsulated Furman's ecumenical spirit:

> His whole temper was sweetened by the spirit of conciliation, and the actions of his life were all of that amiable and obliging character which cements the union of good society. Though naturally grave and thoughtful, he was free from those severities of character which render the more gifted classes of our species

---

4. Brantly, "Extracts from Dr. W. T. Brantly's Sermon Delivered in 1825," 221.
5. Furman, "Rev. Edmund Botsford," 462.
6. Wolever, *Life of John Gano, 1727–1804*, 569–70.

inaccessible. The success of his endeavors in promoting harmony, good order, and amicable feeling, seemed but the result of spontaneous affection.[7]

Richard Furman was known as someone who loved "promoting harmony" and "good order." This firm yet flexible characteristic in his thinking had a profound effect upon Furman's ability to blend modes of thought. He was willing to borrow themes and doctrines from men of all Protestant walks, particularly in Jonathan Edwards's theological tradition. For example, Furman utilized the trademark concepts of "moral ability" and "moral inability" from Jonathan Edwards's *Freedom of the Will*.[8] In his defense of infant salvation, Furman also employed Edwards's idea of natural ability: "By this, we see clearly, that repentance and faith, in fact . . .cannot be the necessary qualifications for admission to the kingdom of God, in persons who have not natural ability to perform them."[9] Furman also encouraged his listeners "to furnish an example of disinterested, generous love," an ideal promoted by Edwards's New England successors.[10] Sometimes Furman sounded like Edwards *and* the Edwardseans when he boasted of "the love of disinterested virtue."[11] Furman was less concerned with upholding every jot and tittle of Calvinism and more concerned with adequately reflecting the truths of the Bible. As a result, his five-point Calvinism was an eclectic blend. Furman sought knowledge and wisdom from all Christians, not simply Calvinists. In a circular letter entitled "On Growth in Grace," Furman advised his readers,

> Read the best books; converse, as you have opportunity, with the wisest and best men; hear the most pious, well-informed, and faithful preachers. Lay yourself open to information: Be willing to have your errors in sentiment and practice corrected; and

---

7. Brantly, "Extracts from Dr. W. T. Brantly's Sermon Delivered in 1825," 215.

8. Furman, "Of Infant Salvation," 592, 596. In *Freedom of the Will*, Jonathan Edwards explained his concept of moral inability in a variety of ways: "A woman of great honor and chastity may have a moral inability to prostitute herself to her slave. A child of great love and duty to his parents, may be unable to be willing to kill his father. A very lascivious man, in case of certain opportunities and temptations, and in the absence of such and such restraints, may be unable to forbear gratifying his lust. A drunkard, under such and such circumstances, may be unable to forbear taking of strong drink" (Edwards, *Works of Jonathan Edwards*, 160).

9. Furman, "Of Infant Salvation," 599.

10. Furman, "Unity and Peace," 305. According to Fitzmier, "disinterested benevolence became the primary chief virtue of Dwight's ethical system" (Fitzmier, *New England's Moral Legislator*, 166). For a treatment of the New Divinity concept of "disinterested benevolence," see Caldwell, *Theologies of the American Revivalists*, 77–83.

11. Furman, "On the Relation the Children of Church Members bear to the Church, and the Duties arising from that Relation," 502.

hearken to the language and evidence of truth, though they may make against your preconceived opinions. Avoid self-conceit, obstinacy of temper, and a fondness for disputation—those invariable evidences of a little mind, and of an unimproved understanding; which are also, when once indulged, almost insurmountable obstacles to true knowledge and wisdom.[12]

Furman drew from theologians of all denominations and styles. In a sermon delivered to the Religious Tract Society in 1816, Furman recommended "writings of Allen, Baxter, Bunyan (as unpolished as he was,) Boston, Doddridge, Stennett, Edwards, Newton, and many others" as a means of conversion.[13] He read from Milton, Young, Pope, Addison, Butler, and others.[14] As a result, Furman "made such progress as would have ranked him among men of the first intelligence in any country." Furman's "studies were chiefly confined to mathematics, metaphysics, belles-lettres, logic, history and theology. He cultivated also an acquaintance with the ancient classics, particularly Homer, Longinus, and Quintillian."[15] Furman was perhaps America's most educated, cosmopolitan Baptist of his time. The peace-making Furman was also well suited to lead the Triennial Convention, a nationwide Baptist convention that brought together Baptists of all kinds, Calvinistic and non-Calvinistic.

In his moderate Calvinism, Furman renovated traditional Calvinistic concepts with ideas that helped him to emphasize the moral responsibility of the sinner. His *Conversion Essential to Salvation* features a spate of Jonathan Edwards's ideas, including sense, light, affections, natural and moral ability, principles, influences, and faculties.[16] The concepts, grammar, and structure of his sermon are nearly identical to those in Edwards's *A Divine and Supernatural Light* (1734).[17] Furman geared much of his theology toward the sinner's duty to repent and believe in the gospel. While affirming the doctrine of total depravity and imputed guilt, Furman did not neglect to emphasize individual responsibility. In a circular letter "On Religious and Civil Duties," Furman exhorted his readers, "Remember your depraved, guilty and lost

---

12. Furman, "On Growth in Grace," 557.

13. Furman, "Conversion Essential to Salvation," 438.

14. Armitage, *History of the Baptists,* 813.

15. Armitage, *History of the Baptists,* 813.

16. According to George Marsden, "the central theme for understanding Edwards—and a theme that raises all the preceding above the merely mundane—is encapsulated in his phrase, 'the divine and supernatural light'" (Marsden, "Quest for the Historical Edwards," 13).

17. Todd, "Influence of Jonathan Edwards on the Missiology and Conversionism of Richard Furman (1755–1825)."

state by nature; remember the vileness and guilt you contracted by actual transgression; and what obligations you are brought under by pardoning, renewing and sanctifying grace."[18] In Furman's mind, humanity was guilty both by Adam's transgression and by its own. His moderate Calvinism was never so inflexible as to nullify the freedom and the duty of the Christian. "Thus all men," Furman opined, "as rational creatures, or voluntary, moral agents, are, because of their obligations and accountability, left utterly inexcusable for their voluntary, sinful actions."[19] With such a consistent emphasis upon the "voluntary" nature of faith, Furman's Calvinism was not fatalistic.

A Legacy of Moderate Calvinism

In some sense, aside from Baptist education and missions, Richard Furman's legacy was tied to moderate Calvinism. He bequeathed his theological flexibility to the next generation of Southern Baptists, each with their own spin on traditional Calvinism. In fact, nearly every Baptist leader whom Richard Furman influenced eventually adopted his "moderate" Calvinistic approach in some way. One of his protégés, William B. Johnson, affirmed the doctrines of total depravity and unconditional election but rejected limited atonement, penal substitution, imputation (in the traditional, distributive sense), and creeds of any kind.[20] In 1848, Johnson boasted to fellow moral governmentalist James S. Mims that most Baptists in South Carolina were "moderate Calvinists."[21] Mims's rejection of imputation had evoked charges of heresy by fellow Furman Academy professor of theology James L. Reynolds (1812–1877). Johnson, the first president of the Southern Baptist Convention, had come vigorously to Mims's defense.

Jesse Mercer, one of the recipients of Furman's Baptist educational fund, also revered Furman.[22] Mercer was a moderate Calvinist whose theology closely mirrored Furman. In his memoir of Mercer, Charles Dutton Mallary framed Mercer's Calvinism in terms strikingly similar to that of Furman:

---

18. Furman, "On Religious and Civil Duties," 547.
19. Furman, "Of Infant Salvation," 595.
20. According to Michael Haykin, Johnson was an "ardent advocate of this governmental view of the atonement, which he appears to have learned from Maxcy when Johnson lived in Columbia between 1809 and 1811" ("Great Admirers of the Transatlantic Divinity," 204).
21. Letter to James S. Mims, March 25, 1848 (William B. Johnson Papers, James B. Duke Library, Furman University); cited in Wills, "*SBJT* Forum: Overlooked Shapers of Evangelicalism," 87.
22. Mallary, *Memoirs of Elder Jesse Mercer*, 99, 411.

> He is rather of the old than of the new school; and inclines to the old fashioned doctrine of free grace, as preached among the Baptists near half a century ago. Though he does not mean to quibble or criticize on mere modes of expression or shades of difference, where the truth is not compromised. He does not fully receive all Mr. Fuller's views of the methods of divine mercy; yet is satisfied with his scheme (as now generally preached, when kept within its own bounds,) as leading to, and finally securing the same great and glorious results, as those of the most approved and (to use a common epithet,) Calvinistic writers of his age.[23]

Mercer was likewise a flexible Calvinist in the mold of Fuller, choosing not to "quibble" over minor distinctions. While adhering to "schemes," he was by no means a systematician. In Mercer's mind, the doctrines of grace,

> when made a party question, and run out into extremes, (to which controversy leads,) it becomes a snare to many souls—a nurse of inaction, and a conductor to the ruins of Antinomianism. The opposite extreme should as assiduously be guarded against. Dwelling on practical religion, and insisting on the duties and obligations of men, without keeping in constant view their moral and guilty disability, and the sovereignty of God in affording salvation to them, as unworthy, helpless sinners, as directly tends to the bogs of Arminianism. The truth of the gospel, rightly held and taught, is that which turns men from darkness to light, and the power of sin to serve the living God, by faith which is in Christ Jesus our Lord.[24]

For Mercer, as for all of Furman's network of moderate Calvinists, the *via media* between Antinomianism and Arminianism was paved with "the truth of the gospel," a single allegiance to *sola Scriptura* to navigate between the Scylla of licentious rationalism and the Charybdis of anthropocentric legalism.

Richard Furman "filled so large a scope" in W. T. Brantly's mind that Brantly even named his second son "Furman Brantly."[25] As another beneficiary of Furman's Baptist fund, Brantly was a moderate Calvinist, but in a different way. Brantly affirmed total depravity and unconditional election, but he rejected limited atonement. For Brantly, all who hear the gospel are

---

23. Mallary, *Memoirs of Elder Jesse Mercer*, 423.

24. Jesse Mercer, "The Doctrines of Grace Favorable to Godliness," in Mallary, *Memoirs of Elder Jesse Mercer*, 322.

25. Brantly, *Saint's Repose in Death*, 23.

actually "included in the atonement."[26] Brantly even pushed back against the traditional Calvinistic notion of irresistible grace. He plainly asserted that "the grace of God as put forth and exerted in the salvation of sinners, is not irresistible."[27] Brantly's views were apparently so provocative that Jesse Mercer, his successor at *The Christian Index,* was forced to come to Brantly's defense and clarify his position.[28] Not surprisingly, Johnson, Mims, Mercer, and Brantly all promoted some form of the moral governmental theory of the atonement.[29] In fact, as Michael Haykin has shown, "moderate" Calvinism was often synonymous with an Edwardsean form of moral governmental theology.[30]

The prominence of moral governmental theory in the nineteenth-century Baptist South was largely due to Richard Furman and his moderate Calvinism. His predecessor Oliver Hart was not as kind to theologians in the Edwardsean tradition. In 1793, Oliver Hart lamented to Furman that Rhode Island College had become a "headquarters" for disseminating "Hopkinsians" or "New Divinity men" into Baptist churches.[31] However, Furman did not seem to mind the Hopkinsian movement. In fact, Furman would seek to fill pulpits with moderate Calvinists from the North. For example, Furman was a "father in the gospel" to Hopkinsian John Waldo and "engaged his strict friendship during life," calling Waldo to preach at the Baptist church in Georgetown, South Carolina.[32] In sharp contrast, the elder Hart celebrated Waldo's eventual rejection as a pastoral candidate from Georgetown in 1793, writing to Furman that he was "glad the Georgetown people have been better taught than to embrace such sentiments or to

26. Brantly, "Original Anecdotes of Dr. Rush," 216.

27. Brantly, *Themes for Meditation, Enlarged in Several Sermons, Doctrinal and Practical,* 59.

28. Jesse Mercer, "My Dear Sister in the Lord," in Mallary, *Memoirs of Elder Jesse Mercer,* 123–25.

29. Mercer defended a form of moral governmental theory similar to Andrew Fuller. He wrote, "I do not mean to contend for the atonement, as a commercial transaction: but I mean to oppose the idea of a vague atonement. I must contend with Fuller that though we cannot view the great work of redemption as a commercial transaction betwixt a debtor and his creditor: yet the satisfaction of justice, in all cases, requires to be *equal* to what the nature of the offense is in reality—and to answer the *same end* as if the guilty party had actually suffered. And for Christ, as our substitute, to have suffered *less* for us than we should if the law had taken its course, would be no atonement at all, and leave us in our sins" (Mallary, *Memoirs of Elder Jesse Mercer,* 290–91; Brantly, "Solitary Hours," Brantly, *Themes,* 159.

30. Haykin, "Great Admirers of the Transatlantic Divinity," 205.

31. Smith, "Order and Ardor," 70; Oliver Hart to Richard Furman, May 30, 1793, Furman MSS.

32. Cook, *Biography of Richard Furman,* 96.

approve of such preaching."[33] In the end, however, Furman would fill the pulpit at Georgetown with like-minded moderate Calvinists. In her history of South Carolina Baptists, Leah Townsend recorded,

> Mr. Furman's labors were so effective as to lead to the constitution of thirty-six members as the Georgetown Church in June 1794, and to its admission into the Charleston Association. William Staughton, a licensed preacher but lately arrived, who assisted Mr. Furman in constituting the church, served as pastoral supply for a year, after which the congregation was without a regular pastor. However, John Waldo, who had come to Georgetown from New York in 1793 as a licentiate and as a teacher in an academy, preached for them until the arrival of Rev. Edmund Botsford in 1797.[34]

Furman had called Staughton from the Baptist Missionary Society and Andrew Fuller's own circle of Particular Baptists. Staughton had been baptized under the ministry of Samuel Pearce in Birmingham, the pastor lauded as the "Baptist Brainerd" and the subject of Andrew Fuller's biographical *Memoirs of the Rev. Samuel Pearce*.[35] Staughton's link to "the seraphic Pearce" was a direct connection from South Carolina to the inner circle of Fuller and the theology of the Baptist Missionary Society, so much that Samuel Lynd boasted that Staughton "was to the Baptist mission cause in this country, what Fuller was among his brethren in England."[36]

Furman also filled classrooms with moderate Calvinists. Jonathan Maxcy, a thoroughgoing Hopkinsian Baptist who defended moral governmental theory, was called from Rhode Island College to be the first president of South Carolina College largely on Furman's recommendation. Through his pen and his politics, Furman was perhaps the leading exponent of moderate Calvinism in the Baptist South. According to Peter Jauhiainen, the theme of moral government "became a hallmark of Hopkinsianism."[37] Though not in an outspoken sense, Furman borrowed heavily from this tradition. However, next to the Bible, his first theological commitment was *The Charleston Confession*.

---

33. Gillette, *Minutes of the Philadelphia Baptist Association, from A.D. 1707 to A.D. 1807*, 256; Oliver Hart to Richard Furman, May 30, 1793, Furman MSS. Although Waldo was rejected as full-time pastor, he did subsequently serve as supply preacher in Georgetown.

34. Townsend, *South Carolina Baptists 1670–1805*, 59.

35. Todd, "Did Jonathan Edwards Help Inspire the Modern Missionary Movement?" 33–47.

36. Lynd, *Memoir of the Rev. William Staughton, D.D.*, 170.

37. Jauhiainen, "Samuel Hopkins and Hopkinsianism," 108.

The Charleston Confession

Richard Furman pastored in an age and in a denomination consumed with questions about Calvinism. Speaking to the diversity of Baptists in America, Brooks Holifield averred, "It would be no exaggeration to say that Baptist theology in America was, for the most part, an extended discussion—and usually a defense—of Calvinist doctrine."[38] Despite his friendly, flexible theology and his supreme commitment to Scripture, Richard Furman's life and ministry were indeed a bulwark of Calvinism. In a letter to Gabriel Gerald in 1797, Furman identified himself with those theologians who have "taken rank with Luther and Calvin, and with Paul, in the work of Reformation."[39] He apparently even conversed with Northern Baptists about the importance of teaching Calvinistic doctrines. In a 1791 letter to Furman, the first president of Rhode Island College (later Brown University), James Manning (1765-1791), lamented the reason to defend Calvinism both in the North and in the South:

> I am sorry there is much occasion to state and defend the great and special doctrines of grace against the insidious attacks of the Methodists and their adherents, more especially in the middle and Southern states—They are scarcely known in New England. With us, the fatal delusion of universal salvation, broached by the infamous John Murray, is the great engine, which the powers of darkness employ to subvert the truth; and in which they have been but too successful, throughout a great part of this country for some years past.[40]

Due to the rise of Methodism and other Arminian forces in the South, Richard Furman was in some sense an apologist for Calvinism. In 1806, he boasted that 130 Calvinistic Baptist churches were established in the state of South Carolina.[41] Furman preached often about humanity's "natural state of guilt" and the "sovereign, discriminating grace of God."[42] According to Furman, the doctrine of original sin "is not viewed by us as opposing the

---

38. Holifield, *Theology in America*, 278.

39. Richard Furman to Gabriel Gerald, Richard Furman Papers, Acc. 1960–016 [Box #1, Folder #11], Special Collections and Archives, Furman University, Greenville, SC.

40. James Manning to Richard Furman, Richard Furman Papers, Acc. 1960–016 [Box #1, Folder #4], Special Collections and Archives, Furman University, Greenville, SC.

41. Cook, *Biography of Richard Furman*, 139.

42. Furman, "Conversion Essential to Salvation," 434; Furman, "Of Infant Salvation," 598.

scriptural doctrine of election, and the divine decrees."[43] Human responsibility for sin and God's providential ordaining of sin were both compatible in Furman's Calvinistic mind. Furman unashamedly affirmed the "sovereign mercy and unchangeable purpose of the promiser."[44]

While Furman rarely ventured to speculate about the order of the divine decrees or the nature of God's intra-Trinitarian counsel, themes like predestination and providence were ubiquitous in his writings, such as in his funeral sermon for President George Washington. Furman chose the text Ps 39:9 ("I was dumb, I opened not my mouth; because thou didst it.") and entitled his sermon "Humble Submission to Divine Sovereignty."[45] In the sermon, Furman depicted the man of God as one who "resigns himself to the sovereign pleasure of God; listening with profound attention, to the imposing dictates of the heavenly mandate, to the voice of Providence, which speaks to man in afflicting dispensations."[46] From the same divine hand came both blessing and affliction. This sovereign figure was the God of Richard Furman. Thus, Furman's ministry was in many ways a defense of Calvinistic soteriology.

Still, in Furman's day, several species of Calvinism flourished among American Baptists. In his magisterial *Theology in America*, E. Brooks Holifield identified four chief varieties of Calvinistic Baptists by the mid-nineteenth century: (1) Baptist Edwardseanism, (2) Fullerite Calvinism, (3) the Calvinism of the Philadelphia Confession, (4) and eclectic populist Calvinism.[47] Typical of many South Carolinians, Richard Furman embodied more than one of these strains. For instance, as will be shown, Furman drew significantly from the theology of Andrew Fuller and even modeled parts of his ministry from Jonathan Edwards. However, in regard to Calvinism, Furman was a confessional Baptist in the Charleston tradition. He was, after all, the pastor of First Baptist Church of Charleston. Aside from the supreme authority of Scripture, Baptist confessionalism served as the primary framework for his entire system of theology.

Under its first pastor, William Screven, FBC Charleston had adopted in substance *The Second London Confession* (1689), a Calvinistic Baptist document modeled after the *Westminster Confession* (1646). *The Philadelphia Confession of Faith* (1742) was an American version of the 1689 document, with the addition of chapters on hymn singing and the laying on of

---

43. Furman, "Of Infant Salvation," 598.
44. Furman, "Constitution and Order," 275.
45. Furman, "Humble Submission to Divine Sovereignty," 367.
46. Furman, "Humble Submission to Divine Sovereignty," 368.
47. Holifield, *Theology in America*, 282.

hands. In 1767, under Furman's predecessor Oliver Hart, the Charleston Association adopted a revision of *The Philadelphia Confession of Faith*, amending only the chapter concerning the laying on of hands. This resultant document was *The Charleston Confession* (1767).[48] Unlike his protégé, William B. Johnson, who believed that confessions of faith were antithetical to biblical authority and gospel simplicity, *The Charleston Confession* served as the scaffolding that framed Furman's theology. *The Charleston Confession* had much to say concerning the atonement, and it profoundly shaped the way Furman conceived of and articulated Christ's atoning work. While *The Charleston Confession* influenced Furman's thinking in ways too many to count in this study, its immediate impact upon his doctrine of atonement can be detected in two primary areas: (1) in his focus upon the atonement as a divine "pardon" that reconciles sinners with God (2) and in his emphasis upon the personal "application" of the atonement through faith. Each of these elements served as a distinctive in the Furmanian atonement.

In order to understand Furman's inheritance from confessional Calvinism regarding the atonement, one must begin with the idea of reconciliation, a theme that featured prominently in Furman's soteriology and one that appears multiple times in *The Charleston Confession*. Reconciliation appears most notably in chapter 8, entitled "Of Christ the Mediator." So critical was reconciliation to his doctrine of atonement that Furman was occasionally willing to treat one concept as nearly equivalent to the other. For instance, in his sermon "Of Infant Salvation," Furman rejoiced that sinners "are freed from condemnation; and joy in God, through their Redeemer, by whom they have received the atonement, or reconciliation."[49] This strong equivalence between atonement and reconciliation was expressed by the language of reconciliation in confessional Calvinism to describe Christ's saving work. Matching *The Second London Confession* verbatim, article 5 of chapter 8 of *The Charleston Confession* reads, "The Lord Jesus by his perfect obedience and sacrifice of himself, which he through the Eternal Spirit once offered up unto God, hath fully satisfied the Justice of God, procured reconciliation, and purchased an Everlasting inheritance in the Kingdom of Heaven, for all those whom the Father hath given unto Him."[50] This vo-

---

48. *The Philadelphia Confession* is the American version of *The Second London Confession* but with the addition of chapters regarding hymn singing and laying on of hands. The only point of difference between *The Philadelphia Confession* and *The Charleston Confession* is the laying on of hands included in the former. *The Charleston Confession* (1767) was reprinted in 1813, 1831, and 1850.

49. Furman, "Of Infant Salvation," 597.

50. *Charleston Confession of Faith*, 8.5.

cabulary is the kind of confessional language that shaped Richard Furman's doctrine of the atonement.

While pecuniary images from *The Charleston Confession* like purchase, value, and inheritance were extremely rare in Furman's writings, forensic and sacerdotal concepts such as satisfaction, justice, sacrifice, intercession, imputation, and reconciliation were far more common. In fact, the latter dominated Furman's doctrine of the atonement. Chief among these themes in Furman's thinking was the concept of reconciliation, which also appears in article 10 of chapter 8 of *The Confession*. It reads, "We need his priestly office to reconcile us and to present us acceptable unto God."[51] When Furman spoke of reconciliation, he was drawing from a well of confessional Calvinism; and like *The Confession*, Furman viewed reconciliation as the fruit of Christ's mediatorial work. For instance, upon considering the "nature and tendency of the gospel," Furman exclaimed, "How clearly does it point out the way of reconciliation and bliss, through the meritorious obedience, complete atonement, and prevalent intercession of a Divine Mediator and Redeemer; and by the sanctifying influence of the Holy Spirit!"[52]

For Furman, reconciliation was also a two-way street. It was a significant facet in the Furmanian atonement because it carried implications for both God and mankind. In his funeral sermon for Oliver Hart entitled "Rewards of Grace Conferred on Christ's Faithful People," Furman preached of the eternal rest of the saints and insisted, "Their reconciled God, who has accepted them through the righteousness and intercession of his son, looks on them with a propitious eye."[53] While reconciliation is accomplished unilaterally by God, both parties—human and divine—are reconciled by the atoning blood of Christ. Sinful human beings are reconciled to God, and they to him. Therefore, in Furman's mind, to be found in Christ is to be a reconciled sinner united with a reconciled God. As a Baptist preacher and faithful Protestant, Furman believed that faith resulted in "immediate reconciliation to God, according to the gospel scheme of salvation."[54]

While Furman strongly associated the theological concepts of atonement and reconciliation, they were not completely synonymous in his mind. In his eulogy of Alexander Hamilton, Furman supplied a more robust definition of reconciliation without explicitly including the word atonement. Once again, like chapter 8 of *The Confession*, Furman viewed reconciliation in the context of Jesus Christ's role as Mediator: "Reconciliation to God,

---

51. *Charleston Confession of Faith*, 8.10.
52. Furman, "America's Deliverance and Duty," 403.
53. Furman, "Rewards of Grace," 333.
54. Furman, "Alexander Hamilton," 236.

through the mediation of his son, comprehends the pardon of our sins, justification of our persons, renovation of our nature, adoption in the heavenly family, and a title to eternal life."[55] In Furman's view, reconciliation was a broad soteriological concept entailing pardon, justification, renovation, adoption, and heavenly title. Furman nearly equated reconciliation with restoration. For Furman, reconciliation encompassed not only right legal standing with God but filial status as well. Reconciliation with God includes reception into his family and all the due benefits as his sons and daughters. Therefore, in some sense, to reconcile is to restore.

Most important for this study, however, is the first concept in Furman's list of benefits entailed in reconciliation, pardon. For Furman, Christ's principal work in the reconciliation of sinners is the act of pardon, a concept that Furman drew from confessional Calvinism. In fact, the concept of pardon is pervasive in the *Charleston Confession*. Unlike the concept of reconciliation, the theme of pardon emerges in several chapters in the *Confession*, including "Of the Fall of Man, of Sin, and of the Punishment Thereof" (6.5), "Of Justification" (11.1, 11.5), "Of Repentance unto Life and Salvation" (15.3), and "Of Good Works" (16.5). With such a heavy confessional presence, Richard Furman inevitably preferred the concept of pardon in his doctrine of atonement, so much so that pardon and atonement were virtually synonymous in his mind.

For instance, as an evangelistic preacher, Furman pleaded earnestly with sinners to trust in Christ's "atoning blood for pardon."[56] As will be shown, Furman upheld the work of Christ in a tripartite scheme that often interchanged the themes of pardon, atonement, and blood. The idea of pardon was central to the gospel in this framework. Furman encouraged his listeners to "apply to him for salvation with reliance on his merit for pardon and acceptance with God."[57] At the very beginning of his sermon entitled "On the Analogy between the Dispensations of Grace by the Gospel, and a Royal Marriage Feast," Furman preached triumphantly: "We see Messiah's Kingdom established among men, in its glory and beauty; and hear the glad tidings which God, through the mediation of his Son, has sent to all mankind; even to the most guilty and wretched, publishing pardon, peace, and salvation."[58] As will be shown, the theme of pardon appealed greatly to Furman due to his conviction that God is the preeminent Lawgiver and Moral Governor of the universe, whose benevolence is depicted best in terms of

---

55. Furman, "Alexander Hamilton," 237.
56. Furman, "Unity and Peace," 307.
57. Furman, "Conversion Essential to Salvation," 429.
58. Furman, "Royal Marriage Feast," 465.

clemency and free grace. Furman utilized this confessional theme to suit his own moral governmental theology.

Application of the Atonement by Faith

The second primary way that *The Charleston Confession* significantly influenced Richard Furman's doctrine of the atonement concerns the personal application of the atonement. For Furman, Christ's atonement was a "complete atonement" in its intrinsic merit; however, it must be appropriated personally to the believer by faith. Furman preferred the language of application, a theme he no doubt borrowed from *The Charleston Confession*. Article 8 of chapter 8 of *The Confession* concerns the communication of grace to the believer,

> To all those for whom Christ hath obtained eternal redemption, he doth certainly, and effectually apply, and communicate the same; making intercession for them, uniting them to himself by his spirit, revealing unto them, in and by the word, the mystery of salvation; persuading them to believe, and obey, governing their hearts by his word and spirit.[59]

The Confession employs the word "apply" in describing the work of Christ as it is communicated to the believer. The application of Christ's atonement was to become an important theme in Furman's preaching and indispensable in the way he harmonized a limited atonement with the universal sufficiency of Christ's atoning blood. Similar to *The Confession*, Furman believed this application was rendered "effectual" by the Holy Spirit. Article 4 of chapter 11 of *The Confession*, entitled "On Justification," similarly states, "God did from all eternity decree to justify the elect, and Christ did in the fullness of time die for their sins, and rise again for their justification; nevertheless, they are not justified personally, until the Holy Spirit doth in time due actually apply Christ unto them."[60] Like *The Confession*, Furman also rejected the doctrine of eternal justification, insisting that the atonement benefits the sinner only when they reach out in faith. Only then is the atonement "applied" in a saving way. As a Calvinist, Furman affirmed that all believers are elected unconditionally from eternity, but they are not properly saved from eternity. Salvation is conditional upon faith in the sense that faith always attends salvation. In other words, while Christ's righteousness is the efficient

---

59. *Charleston Confession of Faith*, 8.8.
60. *Charleston Confession of Faith*, 11.4.

cause of salvation, faith is certainly a condition of salvation in its application of Christ's atonement.

In his exegesis of Rom 4:7–8 ("Blessed are those whose lawless deeds are forgiven, and whose sins are covered; blessed is the man against whom the Lord will not count his sin."), Furman explained the atonement in terms of propitiation and the removal of guilt; but he also insisted that the benefits of Christ must be "applied" through faith:

> This, St. Paul shows, is expressive of justification, and peace with God, through Christ's obedience, and propitiatory sacrifice: the benefits of which are applied to the souls of real penitents and believers. Their guilt, through his atonement, is completely removed; and, by the act of grace, cast, as it were, into the depths of the sea, to be seen or remembered no more.[61]

Richard Furman's words are conformed to the language of *The Charleston Confession*. Words like justification, obedience, sacrifice, and even atonement were familiar terms in Furman's day; but the concept of application was certainly endemic to confessional Calvinism. While tailoring the gospel message to focus upon the importance of repentance and faith (i.e., "real penitents and believers"), Furman remained well within his confessional confines. The concept of application served as a theological tool for Furman in underscoring the necessity of faith for salvation while maintaining the finished work of Christ. According to Furman, Christ's atonement at the cross was a "complete atonement," yet incomplete in the sense that it requires "application" to the soul of the believer in order to secure personal salvation and remove his or her guilt before God.[62] Furman did not believe these two things contradicted in any way. In fact, inevitably, Furman's extended emphasis upon the application of the atonement became a point of departure from classical five-point Calvinism as he coupled this point with an emphasis upon the universal sufficiency of the gospel to save all.

From the application of grace to the concept of pardon so pervasive in his writings, Richard Furman's doctrine of the atonement cannot be understood properly without an evangelistic frame. In a sermon preached at the High Hills of Santee in 1793 entitled "Unity and Peace," Furman implored his audience,

> Have we awoke to the serious consideration of eternal things; to a discovery of our guilt and depravity, and of divine wrath as ready to overwhelm a guilty, impenitent world? Has divine

---

61. Furman, "Conversion Essential to Salvation," 433.
62. Furman, "America's Deliverance and Duty," 403.

mercy also appeared to us in the gospel, and Christ been endeared in all the amiableness of his character and sufficiency of grace? Have we, in the exercise of divine faith, fled for refuge to his mediation; do we trust in his immaculate righteousness for justification before God, and to his atoning blood for pardon?[63]

For Furman, the doctrine of atonement was not an abstract, confessional idea relegated to the classroom. It belonged in the pulpit, and it was most suited for evangelistic invitations to receive the blood of Jesus. While the atonement was the work of Christ, its telos was the faith and salvation of the believer. Furman's doctrine of atonement was therefore consistently and relentlessly toward this end. "It is incumbent on a church," Furman insisted, "to exhibit to her sister churches, as well as to the world at large, a just view of the great doctrines and ordinances of the gospel, in candor and godly simplicity."[64]

Furthermore, Richard Furman's confessional Calvinism was not simply for homiletics. It also extended to the catechesis of children at First Baptist Church of Charleston. Furman held quarterly sessions to teach and quiz anywhere from sixty to one hundred children over the material in Benjamin's Keach's well-known Baptist catechism.[65] Keach was one of the leading signatories of *The Second London Confession* (1689),and his son Elias helped establish several Baptist churches in the Philadelphia Association. Interpreting the work of Christ through a tripartite scheme of prophet-priest-king, Question 29 of the catechism asks, "How does Christ execute the office of a priest?" In turn, the children of FBC Charleston were to reply, "Christ executes the office of a priest, in His once offering up of Himself, a sacrifice to satisfy divine justice, and reconcile us to God, and in making continual intercession for us (1 Pet. 2:24; Heb. 9:28; Eph. 5:2; Heb. 2:17; 7:25; Rom. 8:34)."

Not surprisingly, questions 33 and 34 of the catechism both concern the Spirit's "application" of Christ's redemption through the act of faith. Later, Question 37asks, "What is Justification?" to which the children were to respond, "Justification is an act of God's free grace, wherein He pardons all our sins, and accepts us as righteous in His sight, only for the righteousness of Christ imputed to us, and received by faith alone." The concepts of reconciliation, pardon, and application were to become salient themes in Furman's preaching; and he ensured that his congregants knew these

---

63. Furman, "Unity and Peace," 307.
64. Furman, "Unity and Peace," 299.
65. Baker and Craven, *Adventure in Faith*, 212.

themes from a young age. While each concept had deep roots in confessional Calvinism, Furman made them uniquely his own.

A Liberal Baptist

Richard Furman was a moderate, confessional Calvinist. His Calvinism was confessional enough to hold to all five points of traditional Dortian Calvinism yet loose enough to inject ideas like moral inability and moral government. However, Furman saw himself primarily as a Baptist. As the inaugural president of the Triennial Convention, Furman was a prominent leader in the Baptist world. In all of American Baptist history, perhaps no level of honor was paid to any pastor like the kind William B. Johnson ascribed to Furman.[66] When welcomed to the floor as the fourth president of the Triennial Convention, Johnson paid homage to his predecessor and hero, "the sainted Furman."[67] In his tribute to his mentor, Johnson recalled, "It was no unfrequent remark that, if good works could save a man, the good works of Dr. Furman would assuredly secure *him* admission into Heaven."[68] Moreover, Furman's physical stature seemed to match his social position. "Indeed," Johnson remembered of the Charleston sage, "his very appearance preserved order."[69] Basil Manly Jr., Furman's successor at FBC Charleston, called Furman "the wisest man I ever knew" and described his pastorate as "the most important period" in the history of FBC Charleston.[70] For many, Furman was a Baptist hero. Although he was amicable to brethren of all denominations, Furman staunchly defended the Baptist faith. For example, according to Furman, strict communion was essential to separate Baptists from pedobaptists who chose the "innovation" of infant baptism.[71] As the pastor of the oldest Baptist church in the South, Furman proudly boasted

---

66. According to Tupper, "In the community no minister ever enjoyed so large a share of general confidence and reverence," quoted in King, *History of South Carolina Baptists*, 24. In "Reminiscences," Johnson recalled, "My acquaintance with this man of God began when I was a boy, and I well remember the deep and solemn impression which his grave and ministerial appearance made upon my mind, young as I then was; an impression which was deepened by a more familiar knowledge of his character," quoted in King, *History of South Carolina Baptists*, 212.

67. Woodson, *Giant in the Land*, 98.

68. Johnson, "Richard Furman, D.D.," 13.

69. Johnson, "Richard Furman, D.D.," 14; Johnson also said, "Indeed, so eminent was [Furman] for exemplary piety and holy living, that the whole city held him in veneration. The ungodly stood abashed in his sight, and the profligate carefully hid his iniquities from his view" (13).

70. Rogers, *Richard Furman*, 220; Manly, *Mercy and Judgment*, 52–54.

71. Furman, "On the Communion of Saints," 568–69.

his Baptist identity, but not in a contentious way. He was, like his predecessor Oliver Hart, a "consistent, liberal Baptist."

In a number of ways, Richard Furman stood at the crossroads of Baptist America. As a young preacher, he partnered with those Baptists who had attended the fabled revivals of the Great Awakening. In his funeral sermon for Hart, Furman recalled that his mentor was eighteen years old when he sat "under the ministry of that eminent servant of Christ, Rev. George Whitefield, of the Episcopal Church; of Rev. Messrs. the Tennents, Edwards, and their associates, of the Presbyterian and Congregational Churches; and of the Rev. Abel Morgan, and others, of the Baptist Church."[72] Further still, Furman was shaped profoundly by the American Revolution, an event he also interpreted as divine intervention. On the other hand, his Southern Baptist disciples lived to see his hard-fought union torn asunder in civil war. Furman's life and ministry were epochal, straddling the most important ages in American history.

Furman also stood at an intellectual crossroads. Generationally, he was the spiritual child of Separate Baptist revivalism spawned from the Great Awakening. However, as the first president of the Triennial Convention, he was also at the forefront of a new era of Baptist institutionalism.[73] On one hand, Furman acknowledged the fruits of the Methodist camp meetings in the West, among "some incidental evils."[74] On the other hand, Furman was himself an educated Baptist during a time when most Baptists were not.[75] In the state of South Carolina, "no man except Furman himself had done more for the cause of education."[76] Furman's own educational vision forged the beginnings of The Southern Baptist Theological Seminary, which grew out of the theological faculty at Furman University.[77] In "Three Changes in Theological Institutions," James P. Boyce identified his own approach

72. Furman, "Rewards of Grace," 334–35.

73. Tom Nettles explained, "After having heard Reese preach the Edwardsian conversionism of the Separate Baptists and the believer's baptism of the Baptists, Richard Furman set out to study these issue for himself. Other theological matters also gained his attention as he studied sin, justification, atonement, and grace. He became convinced that the system taught by Reese was the system taught in the Bible" (Nettles, "Richard Furman," 140). On May 16, 1774, when he was eighteen years old, Furman was ordained by Reese and Evan Pugh to be pastor at High Hills.

74. Furman, "Letter to Dr. Rippon," 417.

75. Reynolds, "Life and Work of Richard Furman," 115.

76. Furman, "Letter to Dr. Rippon of London," 416–17; King, *History of South Carolina Baptists*, 172.

77. According to King, both Furman University and The Southern Baptist Theological Seminary "became eventual products of the keen educational concern of Richard Furman" (King, *History of South Carolina Baptists*, 23–24).

with that of Richard Furman: "From the very beginning of Baptist efforts for education in this State to the present moment, this has always been the mainspring of our movements." Boyce praised "that band of worthies of whom but a few remain to counsel us by their wisdom, and to move us to self-abasement by their piety and zeal, in whose minds first originated the idea of Furman Academy."[78] The life of Richard Furman was indeed a linchpin in American Baptist history.

Furman also served as a Baptist portal of sorts from the North to the South, conversant with Northern Baptists and able to draw men from New England to South Carolina. Internationally, Furman served as the Baptist link between English and American Baptists. He corresponded with members of the Baptist Missionary Society and lauded the organization "whose missionaries have fixed the principal seat of their mission at Serampore."[79] Under his leadership, the Triennial Convention supported Adoniram Judson (1788–1850), the first American Baptist missionary stationed in Burma.[80] Furman's works even enjoyed a place in the library of Andrew Fuller.[81] According to James A. Rogers, Furman fulfilled "the role of a leading American Baptist identified with the work of William Carey and the English Baptist missionary initiative."[82] But Furman also stood at the crossroads of Baptist theology. Furman quoted from both John Gill and Andrew Fuller, theologians who have been juxtaposed.[83] He was a Regular Baptist in the mold of *The Charleston Confession*. However, he was influenced also by the theology of Philip Doddridge, Timothy Dwight, and other non-Baptists. Indeed, Richard Furman was a seemingly paradoxical figure. Therefore, naturally, his theology was a bricolage of styles and themes. Furman was a "committed, liberal Baptist," but he was influenced also by the great men and the great ideas of his age.

---

78. Boyce, *Three Changes in Theological Institutions*, 8–9.

79. Furman, "Conversion Essential to Salvation," 437–38.

80. The Triennial Convention also sent out its first missionary, Luther Rice.

81. In Andrew Fuller's diary, he recorded his reading of Furman's *A Sermon, on the Constitution and Order of the Christian Church, Preached before the Charleston Association of Baptist Churches* (Charleston, SC: n.p., 1791). This is included in the appendix of *The Complete Works of Andrew Fuller*, vol. 1, edited by Michael D. McMullen and Timothy D. Whelan.

82. Rogers, *Richard Furman*, 210.

83. Furman, "Constitution and Order of the Christian Church," 267–68; Brantly, "Extracts from Dr. W. T. Brantly's Sermon Delivered in 1825," 224; in *By His Grace and for His Glory*, Thomas J. Nettles attempted to disabuse his readers of the idea that John Gill was a Hyper-Calvinist (79–80).

Major Influences on Furman

Timothy Dwight and the New Divinity

In order to contextualize Richard Furman's doctrine of atonement, the New Divinity is an appropriate starting point. While Furman was a confessional Calvinist, the Edwardsean tradition constituted a theological force nearly as potent in his soteriological thinking. In the year of Furman's death, William T. Brantly delivered a sermon in his honor. Brantly declared, "like Melanchthon he was great in counsel, and whilst conducting plans of general utility and benevolence, exhibited a wisdom, the plenitude of which seemed adequate to the occasion." Brantly then took stock of Furman's most significant influences: "Though in his view of Scripture doctrine he followed no man exclusively, yet he was not unwilling to be found coinciding with such men as Doddridge, Fuller, and Dwight."[84] Remarkably, all three of the theologians Brantly listed were either directly or indirectly affiliated with the theological school known as the New Divinity, a tradition spawned from the theology of Jonathan Edwards. Timothy Dwight, for example, was Jonathan Edwards's grandson and president of Yale University, Edwards's alma mater.[85] Not only did Furman and Dwight share Federalist loyalties and similar aristocratic sensibilities, but each man was known for his emphasis on revival and his *de*-emphasis on harsh theological debate. Just as the missionary endeavors in the Triennial Convention had typified Furman's legacy, a series of student revivals at Yale had done likewise for Dwight.

Most importantly, Furman absorbed at least some of his affinity for the theme of moral government from Timothy Dwight. According to Mark Noll, the trope of moral government, a response to Real Whig discourse in American public life, "began with Bellamy, was developed further by Dwight, and came to prevail everywhere among New Englanders in the generation of Beecher and Taylor."[86] As president of Yale, Dwight was ideally established to disseminate this key theological motif. "In short," Charles Hambrick-Stowe insisted, "Timothy Dwight secured the place of Yale College as the epicenter of an evolving evangelical Calvinist New England

---

84. Brantly, "W. T. Brantly's Sermon," 221.

85. According to Ahlstrom, "As the founder of the New Haven Theology, [Dwight] begins a new trend that was carried to completion by Nathaniel William Taylor. In preferring the Scottish Philosophy to Locke and Berkeley, and in enlarging upon man's moral and intellectual agency, he was certainly not a strict Edwardsean." Ahlstrom, *Religious History of the American People*, 419.

86. Noll, *America's God*, 290–91.

theology."[87] According to Dwight, "Sin is a crime, committed against the Government of God" because, most importantly, "the Government of God over his moral creatures is a moral Government; that is, a Government of rules and motives; or of laws, rewards, and punishments."[88]

As a result, many of Dwight's students became stalwarts for the moral governmental theory of the atonement. Noah Porter, in his introduction to Nathaniel Taylor's *Lectures on the Moral Government of God*, said of Dwight's chief disciple, "The Moral Government of God was the great thought of Dr. Taylor's intellect, and the favorite theme of his instructions in theology. It occupied his mind more than any and every other subject. . . .This object directed all his studies. All his investigations had their starting point from this central theme."[89] While Furman was by no means a New Englander, and he did not study Taylor's New Haven theology, his thinking was defined also by moral government and influenced by Timothy Dwight.

Oliver Crisp identified the theological DNA of Jonathan Edwards in the moral governmental theory of the atonement that prospered during the days of the New Divinity. Though Edwards did not adopt moral governmental theory to the negation of penal substitution, his apparent blending of the two foreshadowed Richard Furman and also gave imprimatur to those Edwardseans who would hold exclusively to moral governmental theory:

> The evidence suggests that the seeds of the New England governmental view of the atonement were sown by Edwards himself. But he did not have the opportunity, or perhaps the inclination, to develop this in his own work. So the views expressed by Bellamy, Samuel Hopkins, and Jonathan Edwards, Jr., to name the three most important exponents of the doctrine among the theologians of the New Divinity, were, one might think, a doctrine innovation in one respect. But they were building on some ideas latent in the work of Edwards Senior, and they did, it appears, have his sanction for doing so.[90]

As a result, Jonathan Maxcy, one of Furman's closest friends, boasted of the "penetrating sagacity of an Edwards, or Hopkins," as if the two men were similar in their theology, though Edwards never elaborated on his moral

---

87. Hambrick-Stowe, "New England Theology in New England Congregationalism," 168.

88. Dwight, *Theology; Explained and Defended in a Series of Sermons*, 2:195–96.

89. Sweeney, *Nathaniel Taylor, New Haven Theology, and the Legacy of Jonathan Edwards*, 91.

90. Crisp, "Moral Government of God," 78–79.

governmental theory in the way that Hopkins did.[91] The strong moral governmental strain among Baptists found its origin in New Divinity theology. Furman partially participated in this tradition in much the same way that Timothy Dwight did but not in an outspoken sense.

Andrew Fuller and Moral Government

Also on Brantly's list of Furman's influences were Philip Doddridge and Andrew Fuller, the latter of whom was also influenced heavily by the New Divinity. Doddridge was Jonathan Edwards's contemporary, and E. P. Clipsham has identified him as an evangelical Calvinist "precursor" to Fuller.[92] Fuller himself deeply influenced Richard Furman in a number of ways. His *Essays* was one of Furman's five all-time favorite books (including the Bible). Furman also corresponded with Fuller's missionary compatriots like Sutcliff, Ryland, and Pierce.[93] Fuller's impact on Furman was seen in their mutual commitment to moral governmental theory. Like Fuller, Furman was a Particular Baptist who attempted to blend theories of the atonement. In 1830, Jesse Mercer, a follower of Andrew Fuller, confirmed that Fuller "contends for the atonement, as made to law and justice, as satisfaction for a crime, and not as payment of a debt," but Fuller "never thought of denying imputation, or even substitution."[94] Mercer's description could have been applied to Furman himself! Furman and Fuller accentuated the same themes in their respective doctrines of atonement, and both men seemed to soft-pedal the idea of substitution. Furman, however, was not so vague on the doctrine of imputation.

The New Divinity influenced Andrew Fuller significantly. Like Richard Furman, Fuller was exposed to the ministry of Timothy Dwight. In 1805, Fuller wrote to Dwight,

> The writings of your grandfather, President Edwards, and of your uncle, the later Dr. Edwards, have been food to me and many others. Our brethren Carey, Marshman, Ward, and Chamberlain, in the East Indies, all greatly approve of them [especially the elder Edwards' works on justification]. . . .Some

---

91. Maxcy, "Funeral Sermon Occasioned by the Death of the Rev. James Manning, D.D.," 151.

92. Clipsham, "Andrew Fuller and Fullerism," 99–114.

93. Brantly, "W. T. Brantly's Sermon," 224; Reynolds, "Life and Work of Richard Furman," 16; Furman, "Miscellaneous Letters," 117.

94. Mercer, *Ten Letters*, 11.

pieces which I have met with of yours have afforded me much pleasure.[95]

Fuller seemed to imbibe much of the theology of Edwards and Edwards's successors. For this reason, examining Andrew Fuller's doctrine of atonement, Jeremy Pittsley has identified "the influence of the New Divinity on his theology."[96] This influence was never more evident than in Fuller's use of moral governmental language to describe the atonement, language that Furman no doubt absorbed in his own writings on the atonement.

Fuller boasted, "Christ having obeyed the law and endured the curse, and so fulfilled the *terms* of his eternal engagement, God can in a way honorable to all his perfections pardon and receive the most guilty sinner that shall return to him in Christ's name."[97] Similar to Furman, Fuller often included themes like pardon, honor, government, and divine perfections. In his work *The Atonement of Christ*, Fuller wrote of the everlasting punishment "required for the due honor of his government to be exercised through the atonement of his beloved Son; that with this sacrifice God is well pleased, and can, consistently with all his perfections, pardon and accept of any sinner, whatever he hath done, who believeth in him."[98] This language is nearly identical to that of Furman, who was prone to contemplate the "perfections and government of the Deity" in almost all of his sermons.[99]

Like Furman, Fuller promoted the idea that the atonement publicly upheld the justice and integrity of God's law while also making a real atonement. "In other words," Paul Brewster explains in *Andrew Fuller: Model Pastor-Theologian*,

> it is possible to retain full belief in the substitutionary nature of Christ's work on the cross for sinners and at the same time allow that God has vindicated his justice in that act. These different models for understanding the atonement can be made complementary and do not have to be seen as standing at cross-purposes.[100]

---

95. "To Timothy Dwight," in *Armies of the Lamb: The Spirituality of Andrew Fuller*, 199–200. Furman aided these same figures (Cary, Marshman, and Ward) in their translation of the Bible for the Baptist Missionary Society. Cook, *Biography of Richard Furman*, 102.

96. Pittsley, "Christ's Absolute Determination to Save," 143.

97. Fuller, "Reply to Mr. Button," 433.

98. Fuller, *Atonement of Christ*, 386.

99. Furman, "On the Use of Reason in Religion," 529.

100. Brewster, *Andrew Fuller*, 164.

In the theology of Andrew Fuller, Furman saw that such a synthesis was sustainable and even preferable. In this sense, Furman's governmental substitutionary model was not altogether unique. Instead, his view found its theological precedents in thinkers such as Jonathan Edwards and his disciple Andrew Fuller.

As leaders in their respective Baptist communities and advocates for missions, Richard Furman and Andrew Fuller were kindred Baptist spirits on opposite sides of the Atlantic. However, as will be shown, Furman's overall view of the atonement also encountered the same dilemma as Fuller's. Each attempted to uphold both penal substitutionary and moral governmental views and did so successfully, but to the slight compromise of both doctrines. Fuller has been criticized for his attempt to fuse both views. According to Gerald Priest, "Fuller seems to be expressing a penal satisfaction, but he uses non-penal language, overcompensating for his opposition to a pecuniary sacrifice. He uses, instead, governmental, moral expressions which give the overtone of a Grotian atonement."[101] Others, like Thomas J. Nettles, have taken a more favorable perspective: "Fuller's use of governmental language did not involve him in the mistakes of governmentalists; the atonement never became merely symbolic justice, but maintained its character as an act of actual justice."[102]

Regardless, Fuller's attempt to meld penal substitutionary and moral governmental theories involved him in no small amount of controversy, especially after amending the second edition of his *Gospel Worthy of All Acceptation* to account for his moral governmental views. In order to promote moral governmental themes, Fuller downplayed the traditional idea of imputation and substitution while Furman, a far less systematic thinker, chose not to emphasize the idea of substitution or any commercial themes of the atonement. Neither forsook penal substitution or moral governmental theories. However, compared with James P. Boyce or William B. Johnson, neither offered the most pristine form of their respective systems. Like Furman, Fuller also de-emphasized the commercial nature of the atonement. As Chris Chun has shown, Fuller denied a "strict equivalence" between the atonement and a commercial transaction while remaining "within the boundaries of both commutative and distributive framework in that Christ's satisfaction, which is equal payment of the debt (commutative), and the basis for the classical forensic justification (distributive)."[103] In *The Deity of Christ Essential to Atonement*, Fuller wrote,

---

101. Priest, "Fuller on the Atonement," 145.
102. Nettles, *By His Grace and for His Glory*, 128.
103. Chun, *Legacy of Jonathan Edwards in the Theology of Andrew Fuller*, 166.

> If God requires less than the real demerit of sin for an atonement, then there could be no satisfaction made to Divine justice by such an atonement and though it would be improper to represent the great work of redemption as a kind of commercial transaction betwixt a creditor and his debtor, yet the satisfaction of justice in all cases of offence requires that there be an expression of the displeasure of the offended, against the conduct of the offender, equal to what the nature of the offence is in reality.[104]

Few expositions of the atonement more closely align with Richard Furman's view than this. Like Fuller, Furman believed that the atonement was not primarily about commutative justice, wherein Christ exchanges a good *quid pro quo* with an offended God. Instead, Christ makes satisfaction to divine justice by bearing a penalty equivalent to that incurred by human sin. Furman did not deny the commercial nature of the atonement but subordinated this theme to that of satisfaction of a crime, like Fuller. In a letter to a friend explaining the heresy of Socinianism, Furman explained, "But certain it is, though Christ wrought out the work of redemption alone, he, representatively and virtually, comprehended his people therein, and they may be said to have given satisfaction to justice by the obedience and sufferings he rendered as their surety."[105] While Furman's moral governmental scheme did not allow him to draw a "strict equivalence" between the atonement and a commercial transaction, the Furmanian atonement still satisfied some form of commutative justice. Richard Furman's doctrine of atonement was, in many ways, the American counterpart to Andrew Fuller's. The main point of departure between the two was the doctrine of imputation, as Furman did not shy away from teaching the idea around every turn. According to Furman, "the whole tenor of Gospel doctrine" was that sinners "are accepted of God through the beloved Redeemer, and through the Imputation of his righteousness and atonement."[106]

Social and Political Influences

In addition to theologians such as Timothy Dwight and Andrew Fuller, other social and political factors had significant influence on Richard Furman's view of the atonement. Chief among these cultural influences was the

104. Fuller, *Deity of Christ*, 3:693.

105. Richard Furman Papers, Acc. 1960–016 [Box #1, Folder #11, 34], Special Collections and Archives, Furman University, Greenville, SC.

106. Richard Furman Papers, Acc. 1960–016 ["Saints in Heavenly Rest," 12], Special Collections and Archives, Furman University, Greenville, SC.

widely-used theme of honor. Honor was not only a New Divinity theme; it was especially dominant for Furman's revolutionary era and his milieu in the American South. In Furman's South Carolina, honor was a ubiquitous theme. In his standard work *Southern Honor*, Bertram Wyatt-Brown demonstrates the pivotal significance of honor in Southern behavior and society. He explains,

> Apart from a few lonely dissenters, Southern whites believed (as most people do) that they conducted their lives by the highest ethical standards. They thought that they had made peace with God's natural order. Above all else, white Southerners adhered to a moral code that may be summarized as the rule of honor. Today we would not define as an ethical scheme a code of morality that could legitimate injustice—racial or class. Yet so it was defined in the Old South. The sources of that ethic lay deep in mythology, literature, history, and civilization. It long preceded the slave system in America. Since the earliest times, honor was inseparable from hierarchy and entitlement, defense of family blood and community needs.[107]

Furman's defense of slavery is an obvious indication that he abided by many of the social mores of his Southern community.[108] Honor was a tremendously motivating force in the early and mid-nineteenth century, and it was inculcated into Southerners early on. Recalling his mother's ill-fated departure for Charleston when he was a boy, the fatherless Andrew Jackson remembered her last words to him: "Sustain your manhood always."[109] The world of male honor pervaded the American South. However, for Furman, honor was not simply a social value; it was also deeply theological.

The conversion of Ann Hasseltine Judson (1789–1826) provides an excellent example of the influence of the New Divinity upon evangelicals in Furman's generation, particularly in its emphasis upon the moral idea of honor. Ann and her husband Adoniram, the first American Baptist overseas missionaries, were both adherents to the New Divinity.[110] In her account, young Hasseltine mentions reading Joseph Bellamy's *True Religion Delineated*, widely regarded as the clearest presentation of moral governmental

---

107. Wyatt-Brown, *Southern Honor*, 3–4.

108. Furman, *Exposition of the Views of the Baptists, Relative to the Coloured Population of the United States*.

109. Quoted in Sellers, *Market Revolution*, 176.

110. Furman knew Mr. and Mrs. Judson as friends. In his "Address of the Convention" in Philadelphia, Furman lists them by name and reports on their work "at Rangoon." Furman, "Address of the Convention," 447; Anderson, *To the Golden Shore*, 5, 9–10, 53.

theory in early modern America. Written by one of Jonathan Edwards's two primary disciples, *True Religion Delineated* was actually prefaced by Edwards himself. Hasseltine also records her reading of the recently-published biography on Samuel Hopkins, Edwards's other chief disciple and promoter of moral governmental theory. Hopkins's *System of Doctrines* was widely regarded as the codification of New Divinity beliefs. Hasseltine also read works by Edwards himself and by Philip Doddridge, both of whom Furman references in his writings.

"I felt that if Christ had not died," Hasseltine conjectured, "to make an atonement for sin, I could not ask God to dishonor his holy government so far as to save so polluted a creature, and that should he even now condemn me to suffer eternal punishment, it would be so just that my mouth would be stopped."[111] As examined earlier in this study, the concept of honor was integral to the moral governmental view of the atonement. In this view, Christ's work was a restoration of divine honor after sin had dishonored the Lawgiver and his law. Ultimately, the penitent Hasseltine pens these last words in her journal:

> But though my heart is treacherous, I trust that I have some evidence of being a true Christian; for when contemplating the moral perfections of God, my heart is pleased with, and approves of, just such a Being. His law, which once appeared unjust and severe, now appears to be holy, just, and good. His justice appears equally glorious as his mercy, and illustrative of the same love to universal happiness. The way of salvation by Christ appears glorious, because herein God can be just, and yet display his mercy to the penitent sinner.[112]

The language contained in Hasseltine's conversion narrative is strikingly similar to that of Furman. Furmanian ideas such as moral government, honor, moral perfections, and an emphasis upon the law of God are all shared by Hasseltine, indicating a common theological tradition of some kind. These themes composed the language of the New Divinity. But they were also characteristic of the Revolutionary era.

Did the relationship between honor and morality have special significance for Americans during Furman's generation? Why did the motif of honor prove to be so pervasive in the late eighteenth and early nineteenth centuries? How did this affect the way that early modern theologians discussed the work of Christ? In his recent work *American Honor*, Craig Bruce Smith contends that the idea of honor underwent a moralizing

---

111. Knowles, *Memoir of Mrs. Ann H. Judson, Late Missionary to Burmah*, 18.
112. Knowles, *Memoir of Mrs. Ann H. Judson, Late Missionary to Burmah*, 30.

transformation in the early republic from its days in patriarchal England. No longer was honor assigned by such things as class or status or caste; rather it was earned with virtue and character. In other words, honor was no longer a "descending" concept. Instead it "ascended" with the moral fiber of an individual, regardless of social rank. This kind of social mobility was a radical transition in Anglo-American society. According to Smith, "Honor as an ethical concept pervaded the early republican professional world, with a focus on moral character and merit overtaking the older models of patronage and hierarchal status."[113]

Put simply, during Richard Furman's generation, honor became an increasingly moral concept detached from the idea of power or authority. Therefore, when theologians made reference to divine honor, they were speaking to God's goodness as much as to God's greatness. The atonement was a moral event with God's honor at his conceptual center. When Christ died for the good of the moral universe, he was dying for honor. Smith explains, "The virtuous actions of the individual alone could make them esteemed as honorable, not the deeds of their parents. Honor was simply the public validation of a virtuous life."[114] In this kind of American honor society, Richard Furman applied the best attributes of republican leadership to Jesus Christ, the public servant-leader.

Honor and liberty were also related ideas during the revolutionary era. Elsewhere Smith explains,

> Honor required freedom and independence in order to exist; to remove them made a person a slave, a status that, in the eighteenth century, was widely considered devoid of any form of honor. During the years leading up to the American Revolution, Americans continually linked the ideas of honor and virtue with liberty, freedom, and independence; in many ways, these ideas became inseparable and have only been distanced in the linguistics of the modern era.[115]

This link between honor and freedom is one of the reasons why Furman commonly linked honor to both the atonement of Christ *and* the American cause of liberty against the British. While these were widely different concepts, in Furman's mind, they both occupied the same moral sphere. Speaking of the "rights and privileges" of Americans and the "civil and religious" liberties they enjoy, Furman weaved together redemptive and political themes. In his funeral sermon for George Washington, Furman

113. Smith, *American Honor*, 188.
114. Smith, *American Honor*, 26.
115. Smith, *American Honor*, 69.

reasoned, "Let it not be said, that after his death, Americans have become indifferent to that cause which lay so near to his heart; on his labors in which heaven so propitiously smiled—That cause which is so essential to our present happiness, and as favorable to our future hopes—That cause which is intimately connected with the honor of God, and the interests of the Redeemer's kingdom."[116]

Perhaps most revealing of the moral connotation Furman attached to honor was his negative view of dueling. Interestingly, Furman's sense of honor was incompatible with the practice so often associated with the defense of personal honor. In a sermon on Ps 89:48 delivered after the death of Alexander Hamilton, who was famously killed in a duel with Aaron Burr (the grandson of Jonathan Edwards), Furman concluded his thoughts on Hamilton with a firm denunciation of the deadly sport. He asked rhetorically, "How much precious blood has it been the means of shedding? Of how many valuable citizens has it deprived the nation? What a spirit of resentment, and false honor, has it promoted in the community at large?"[117] In Furman's view, the honor won in dueling was a "false honor." The immorality and turpitude of the practice negated any seeming bravado or public image that could be gained from victory in such a "cruel custom."[118] Killing another person for the sake of honor, in Furman's eyes, was itself dishonorable because it did not reflect the self-sacrifice consistent with true honor. Furman asked,

> Hard, indeed, must be the heart of that man, who from a principle of resentment, for some comparatively small injury done to his honor, can consent to plunge a fellow creature into everlasting ruin, or to quit his own station of duty, assigned by providence, and his eternal hopes, to gratify the inhuman passion. What injury, indeed, to his honor can an individual sustain, in this short life, which will justify the conduct?[119]

That which Furman abhorred is what historian Wyatt-Brown calls "primal honor," or the act of avenging a slight to one's honor through physical force.[120] The latter was utterly dishonorable in Furman's mind because it

---

116. Furman, "Humble Submission to Divine Sovereignty," 382. Furman's relationship to Washington was one of adoration and the utmost respect.

117. Furman, "Eulogy of General Alexander Hamilton," 245. Furman does not appear to have had a special relationship with Hamilton other than their mutual Federalist politics.

118. Furman, "Eulogy of General Alexander Hamilton," 245.

119. Furman, "Eulogy of General Alexander Hamilton," 245–46.

120. Wyatt-Brown, *Southern Honor*, 25.

subordinated the honor of God to one's own fleshly whims. According to Craig Bruce Smith, "Dueling did not define honor culture. A great portion of the Revolutionary generation would come to view dueling as thoroughly dishonorable."[121] Influential leaders such as Richard Furman, with the full force of the gospel, worked to exonerate godly honor against its worldly counterfeits. Smith explains, "Contrary to the popular opinion that dueling was a Southern phenomenon, the specter of the Hamilton-Burr duel even loomed so large that some pro-dueling Southerners were turned against the practice as a matter of honor."[122]

The critical piece to Furman's theology of honor, and the reason he so detested the practice of dueling, is godly virtue. In his sermon at Alexander Hamilton's death, Furman again asked, "Is it the proper test of refined sentiment and virtuous honor? Why, then, are duelists so often charged, and apparently, in justice, with such a variety of immoral, dishonorable actions; while others who are utterly averse to the practice, are deservedly esteemed, confided in, and revered, for their virtue and refinement."[123] For Furman, true honor was "virtuous honor," or honor gained by virtue. The honor that Furman ascribed to Christ, and the honor restored to God in Christ's atoning work, was typified by this sense of benevolence and virtue. In *The Radicalism of the American Revolution*, Gordon Wood explains, "The virtue that classical republicanism encouraged was public virtue." He continues, "Public virtue was the sacrifice of private desires and interests for the public interest. It was devotion to the commonweal."[124] In this sense, Furman conceived of God in terms of the republican civic leader. Moreover, the idea of disinterestedness was embodied in a crucified Christ dying for sinners on a cross. Therefore, when Furman wrote of "a due regard to the honor of God," he was alluding to the humble, loving character of God as much as to his sovereign power.

Richard Furman was a moderate, confessional Calvinist and a consistent, liberal Baptist. However, he was also subject to his own time and place. More than any others, these theological, social, and political factors help explain how Furman integrated the doctrine of moral government into the traditional Calvinistic doctrine of atonement.

---

121. Smith, *American Honor*, 212.
122. Smith, *American Honor*, 220.
123. Furman, "Eulogy of General Alexander Hamilton," 246.
124. Wood, *Radicalism of the American Revolution*, 104.

3

Furman's Two-Part Doctrine of Atonement

Penal Substitutionary Atonement

Imputation

DECADES AFTER FURMAN'S DEATH, the institution bearing his last name, Furman University, was a flourishing Baptist institution with a theology faculty. However, by the mid-nineteenth century, controversy over the atonement had somewhat stained the reputation of the department. James S. Mims (1817–1855), professor of theology, openly rejected the doctrine of imputation—both of Adam's sin to humanity and of Christ's righteousness to believers.[1] These beliefs were characteristic of a theological school at the time known as the New Divinity, of which Furman himself was influenced but not completely. William B. Johnson rushed to defend Mims. Former Furman Academy professor Jesse Hartwell Sr. even wrote Johnson that he believed the "views on 'Imputation' presented by Prof. Mims to be scriptural and correct" and that he had taught the same views openly at Furman.[2] However, the rest of the theology faculty at Furman upheld the more traditional Calvinistic faith upon which the school itself was founded. James L. Reynolds, Mims's chief opponent and accuser, rushed to defend the doctrine of imputation by invoking Richard Furman's doctrine of atonement: "The doctrine of imputed righteousness . . . was held firmly and constantly by our fathers . . . it pervades their writings and is freely expressed

---

1. Haykin, "Great Admirers of the Transatlantic Divinity," 205.
2. Quoted in Randall et al., *Baptist Identities,* 149.

in their hymns . . . it was taught to their children in catechisms . . . as the indisputable truth of God, and therefore a part of our denomination's faith."[3] Richard Furman's name was quite clearly associated with the doctrine of imputation. For this reason, imputation is a reasonable starting place for Furman's doctrine of the atonement.

Despite his moderate Calvinism and his moral governmental views, Richard Furman clearly affirmed the idea of imputation. It was integral to his doctrine of atonement. According to Furman, the "whole tenor of Gospel Doctrine" included "the imputation of [Christ's] righteousness and atonement."[4] Although imputation and atonement were logically distinguishable in Furman's mind, they could never be separated. Christ's imputed (reckoned or accounted) righteousness to the believer and his satisfaction of divine justice on the cross were theologically linked. Together these two things served as the primary lens through which Furman understood the gospel. While these were not the only features of the atonement that Furman emphasized, they were nevertheless two of the most significant components of the Furmanian atonement.

For Furman, imputation was a forensic term. Christ's righteousness is accounted or "imputed" to the believer on the basis of Christ's sinless life under the law. By faith, sinners freely receive his righteousness apart from any merit of their own. Furman believed that Jesus Christ was stricken by the Father *as if* he were unrighteous and believers rewarded *as if* they were righteous. The vicarious nature of the atonement is hinged upon the idea of imputation, wherein the sinner is accounted or declared righteous without being intrinsically so. The basis for Furman's doctrine of justification is imputed, not inherent, righteousness. The guilty sinner is justified as if in a court of law or before a tribunal. The ground of the believer's acceptance before God is not his or her own righteousness but the righteousness of Christ which is now imputed to the sinner by faith.

However, while Furman clearly affirmed imputation, he did not usually speak of an imputation of sin. Instead, he emphasized the imputation of Christ's righteousness, given as a gift to the believer. For example, in his circular letter entitled "On Growth in Grace," Furman boasted, "we are accepted through his intercession, not for our own, but his righteousness, which is imputed to all those who believe in him."[5] On other occasions, Furman explained the concept of righteousness with biblical imagery that

---

3. Reynolds, "On Imputation—No. VIII," 616. Reynolds also cited Baptist Andrew Fuller and other non-Baptist theologians such as Francis Turretin, Charles Hodge, and James H. Thornwell.

4. Furman, "Saints in Heavenly Rest."

5. Furman, "On Growth in Grace," 553–54.

underscored the forensic nature of imputation. For instance, in his sermon to the Marine Bible Society of Charleston, Furman describes the "economy of grace" as an arrangement whereby "this righteousness of the Son of God is imputed to those who believe in him, for their acceptance and justification, in Jehovah's presence. This seems to be intended by the robe of righteousness, of which, the Prophet Isaiah speaks; and by the wedding garment, mentioned in this parable."[6] Contrary to traditional Roman Catholic doctrine and consistent with Reformed Protestant teaching, Furman did not affirm an inherent righteousness in the believer but an adorned righteousness on his or her behalf. In other words, like the sartorial imagery in the Bible, Furman conceived of righteousness as something bestowed upon believers and not necessarily inside the believers themselves.

Furman expounded the doctrine of atonement with the biblical concepts of righteousness and justification. Justification and atonement were, in some sense, two sides of the same soteriological coin. Therefore, Richard Furman preferred to think of imputation in terms of Christ's righteous life and the atonement in terms of Christ's death. In other words, the imputation of Christ's righteousness to the believer is something that resulted in what Furman called justification. On the other hand, the counting of the believer's sin to Christ on the cross resulted in something Furman called atonement. While Furman never spoke in detail of an imputation of sin and he shied away from the language of substitution, he clearly understood the atonement as the counterpart to justification by Christ's righteousness. In a letter to Oliver Hart in 1789, Furman referred to "justification by the righteousness of Christ and atonement through the shedding of his blood."[7] The cross was the epicenter of the Furmanian atonement.

Because Furman downplayed the idea of substitution, his was not the traditional penal substitutionary view. By maintaining that Christ endured the penalty of the law for the individual sinner, Furman operated within the boundaries of a substitutionary model, but his emphasis lay more with the satisfaction of justice than with any kind of exchange of righteousness. When unbelievers languished in a state of guilt, Furman lamented that they lacked an "atonement that it can make to propitiate the Divine Majesty, and procure deliverance from the dreadful curse of his violated Law, which declares 'The soul that sinneth shall die:' so that unless, by sovereign mercy, it is interested in the Mediator's righteousness and atonement, it must remain

---

6. Furman, "Analogy of Grace by the Gospel, and a Royal Marriage Feast," 471.

7. Furman, "Richard Furman to Oliver Hart." Furman then claimed that these tenets of the faith "have been adopted by almost all reformed churches."

under the curse, and perish."[8] Furman's use of the word "propitiate" suggests that he understood sin to be an offense against God as well as against his law. Therefore, Christ's death is a satisfying of divine anger. His blood placates a holy Deity. Christ's atonement gains the favor of God by meeting the demands of the law which were violated by the sinner. In this sense, Christ is a substitute for the believer but not necessarily in a *quid pro quo* sense. Rather, the atonement is a substitutionary aversion of divine punishment, equivalent to the offense committed by sin.

Furman's penal substitutionary model of the atonement also centered around the idea of Christ's obedience. This is where the concepts of justification and atonement come together. By virtue of his sinless life and his pascal death upon the cross, Christ is doubly obedient. Christ's obedient life becomes the basis for his atoning work on the cross. If the attribute of righteousness was integral to Furman's doctrine of imputation, the idea of obedience was inextricable from his conception of righteousness. While Jesus vicariously suffered for the elect upon the cross in order to endure the just punishment of God's law, this punishment composed only half of Christ's earthly obedience. For Furman, Christ alone is righteous because He alone kept the law during his lifetime. In this way, Christ's life as well as his death formed the basis for his atonement. He insisted,

> The all-sufficiency of the Savior's merit, including the suitableness of his mediatorial character and office; the perfection of his righteousness he has wrought out for us, in the obedience to the divine law; and fullness of that satisfaction he has rendered to its penal demands, by suffering the punishment due to sin, whereby he has made a complete atonement for his redeemed.[9]

As Mediator between God and man, Christ merited a "complete atonement" for sinners by fully obeying the divine law in perfect righteousness and by making satisfaction for sin by his sufferings.[10] His obedience is twofold, achieving "perfection" under the standard of the law. This is what Furman means when he references Christ's atonement as a "complete atonement." There is no need to add to Christ's work in any way. He lives and dies for sinners. Jesus Christ has fully satisfied the demands of the law on the cross, and his righteousness is imputed to the believer in such a way that the sinner is accounted as one who has fully kept the law. While the essence of

---

8. Furman, "Royal Marriage Feast," 470.

9. Furman, "Of Growth in Grace," 553.

10. This conception of Christ's twofold obedience is similar to Benjamin Keach's distinction between Christ's "active" and "passive" obedience. Vaughn, "Benjamin Keach," 57.

the atonement is meted out on the cross, it encompasses both the life and death of Christ. The demands of the law are "penal," indicating once again that Furman operated within the boundaries of penal substitutionary atonement. Although he never spoke directly of an exchange between Christ and the believer, he underscored the penalty due to sin which Christ in fact "renders" to God.

Christ's twofold obedience is a concept that Furman absorbed explicitly from the *Charleston Confession*. In article 1 of chapter 11 "On Justification," the *Confession* states that believers receive their righteousness "by imputing Christ's active obedience unto the whole law, and passive obedience in his death for their whole and sole righteousness by faith, which faith they have not of themselves; it is the gift of God."[11] Most confessional Baptists in the American South were familiar with this binary framework. Tom Nettles attests to the theme of Christ's twofold obedience when he asserts, "Furman conceived of Christ as bearing, in His passive obedience, the actual punishment due to sinners, by which action they are forgiven; and as gaining, by His active obedience, the righteousness of the law, the imputation of which constitutes their justification."[12] Furman's doctrine of imputation and thus his doctrine of atonement were founded upon the righteous, twofold obedience of Christ.

Covenant Theology

While imputation was central to Furman's doctrine of the atonement, the penal substitutionary nature of the atonement was but one layer in a larger covenantal framework in Richard Furman's soteriology. Furman's covenant theology provides perhaps the best evidence that he understood the atonement in substitutionary terms, even though he did not emphasize the idea of substitution *per se*. In this covenant framework, Christ stands in the place of sinners because He is appointed by the Father to be the head of a particular people under a particular covenant made between God and man. As a "public head," Christ is an Adamic figure who represents His people.[13] He is, according to Furman, the "Antetype of Adam."[14] Just as Adam's disobedience merits the death of humanity, Christ's obedience merits righteousness for those who would believe. Furman's doctrine of imputation was built

---

11. *Charleston Confession of Faith*, 11.1.
12. Nettles, "Richard Furman," 152.
13. Furman, "Of Infant Salvation," 592.
14. Furman, "Of Infant Salvation," 592.

upon this kind of biblical symmetry and Christ's appointed identity as the second Adam:

> Divine Sovereignty, in connection with justice (and, undoubtedly, with all the attributes of Deity,) has, in bringing them into existence from the mass of fallen human nature, entailed on them the guilt and depravity of Adam; who, as the common Father and representative of mankind, had at this creation, while in innocence, under the covenant of works, the whole of that nature comprehended in himself. That same sovereignty, in union with mercy, appears glorious, in providing for the fallen, helpless creatures, an all-sufficient, gracious Savior, under the character of the second Adam.[15]

Furman understood God and Adam to have undertaken a compact upon creation known as the "covenant of works." Under this covenant, after a probationary period in the Garden, Adam's obedience merited an infinite reward or his disobedience an infinite punishment for he and his descendants. In God's design, according to his sovereignty and his justice, mankind inherited Adam's guilt. Conversely, according to God's mercy, the church inherits grace and righteousness from its head and savior Jesus Christ. Furman's doctrine of atonement was built upon this kind of symmetrical understanding of history.

Furman's covenant theology exhibited a similarity to his Puritan forebears, both American and English. Even when covenantal language was not explicit, the concept of headship undergirded the Puritanical understanding of salvation history. Men like the Connecticut River Puritan Thomas Hooker (1586–1647) insisted that Adam "represented all mankind (as a Parliament man doth for the whole country) for all that should be born of him; so that look what Adam did, all his posterity did."[16] Elsewhere, the language of covenant was more conspicuous, as when Edmund Calamy (1600–1666) maintained that Adam received a "Covenant both for himself and all his posterity. . . .He breaking that Covenant brought not only guilt upon himself but upon all his posterity with him."[17] This covenantal framework stretched back even to pre-Puritan days. Peter Lillback has posited that, despite arguments to the contrary, John Calvin employed the concept of covenant to a significant degree.[18] Even so, whether Lillback's thesis is correct, Henrich Bullinger (1504–1575) has traditionally been recognized

---

15. Furman, "Of Infant Salvation," 594.
16. Quoted in Ball, *Chronicling the Soul's Windings*, 82.
17. Calamy, *Two Solemne Covenants Made between God and Man*, 2.
18. Quoted in Ball, *Chronicling the Soul's Windings*, 75.

as the first to systematize and legitimize covenant theology. The disciple and successor of Ulrich Zwingli in the Zurich church, Bullinger elaborated upon this theology in works like *Decades*. According to J. Wayne Baker, Bullinger's influence upon the Marian exiles was one of the primary ways in which covenantal thinking on the continent permeated English Puritanism. His theology shaped those Puritans "especially like Preston, who were the fount of New England covenant thought."[19] Thus, Furman's covenantal theology found its ancestry in sixteenth-century Europe by way of seventeenth-century England and New England.

The prelapsarian covenant known as the covenant of works was yet another concept that Furman had in common with *The Charleston Confession*. In chapter 20, entitled "Of the Gospel, and the Extent of the Grace Thereof," article 1 reads, "The covenant of works being broken by sin, and made unprofitable unto life, God was pleased to give forth the promise of Christ, the seed of the woman, as the means of calling the elect, and begetting in them faith and repentance."[20] Furman understood God's first covenant with humanity as a broken legal contract. While the effects of Adam's fall can be felt universally by all of his sinful progeny, the covenant no longer offers life for any of his children. For this reason, a newer, gracious covenant was made with the elect in Christ, the God-man. Like the law, the covenant of works cannot supply fallen humanity with a righteousness of its own. Chapter 19 of the *Confession* is entitled "Of the Law of God," and the sixth article reads, "Although true believers be not under the law as a covenant of works, to be thereby justified or condemned, yet it is of great use to them as well as to others."[21] Furman made this same distinction between the law and the covenant of works. The covenant of works continues in effect for all of Adam's offspring, condemning every sinner under the just law of God. However, never does Furman equate the covenant and the law directly as if they were somehow interchangeable concepts.[22]

For Furman, the covenant is an agreement of terms between God and Adam of which the moral law was binding. This law was, according to Furman, the essence of the Mosaic law.[23] Due to Adam's disobedience under the moral law revealed in creation, Furman affirmed that God brought all of humanity "into existence from the mass of fallen human nature" and that

---

19. Baker, *Heinrich Bullinger and the Covenant*, 166.

20. *Charleston Confession of Faith*, 20.1.

21. *Charleston Confession of Faith*, 19.6.

22. For instance, English Puritan Francis Roberts (1609–1675) argued that the "Moral Law is the Covenant of Works" (Roberts, *Mysterie and Marrow of the Bible*, 19).

23. Furman, "On Covetousness," 575.

he "entailed on them the guilt and depravity of Adam."[24] As the physical progeny of Adam, every human being is born sinfully depraved and stands guilty before God. Furman's belief in the imputation of Adam's sin to the world is built upon his covenant theology. While Furman did not usually emphasize imputation of sin as he did the imputation of Christ's righteousness, his understanding of the covenants was consistent with a concept of double imputation. Because of Adam's sin, God "entails" sin and guilt upon his descendants just as he bestows Christ's righteousness upon the elect.

Contrary to the claims of some paedobaptists, Furman believed that the doctrine of original sin did not impugn believer's baptism; rather it supported it. In his mind, apart from God's sovereign grace in the gospel itself, no church covenant has the power to change the heart of the sinner. In a circular letter entitled "The Relation Children of Church Members Bear to the Church," Furman takes note of the common sinfulness of all children, even those raised by godly parents. According to Furman, "the depravity and guilt of human nature" is "frequently evinced to our observation, in the children of truly pious parents, who prove notoriously wicked, and finally impenitent; notwithstanding all the care of education, and the solicitude of their parents to impress them with a just sense of religion."[25] Furman's Baptist convictions rested upon a deep sense of the sinfulness of mankind and the exclusive authority of the gospel to save and transform the children of Adam.

Furman called Adam the "common Father and common representative of mankind," indicating both a natural and federal understanding of headship in Furman's soteriology. Furman labels Adam "our fallen progenitor" as well as the "representative" of mankind, effectively making Adam responsible for the fallenness of his children as both the first human and as the appointed head of his race.[26] Consequently, Adam's offspring sinned in his sinning. According to Furman, all of human nature is "comprehended in himself." In other words, Furman understood every sinner to have sinned when Adam transgressed in the Garden by virtue of being "in" Adam, their father and representative.

On the other hand, in this same covenantal framework, Furman understood Jesus Christ to be the representative of a new humanity juxtaposed with fallen humanity in the line of Adam. In his exegesis of Romans chapter 5, Furman concludes,

---

24. Furman, "Of Infant Salvation," 594.
25. Furman, "Relation Children of Church Members Bear to the Church," 488.
26. Furman, "Of Infant Salvation," 594.

> we see 1st Adam, the first man, and Father of the Human Race; and our Lord Jesus Christ, represented as public heads of mankind; and placed in contrast. . . .The first, as the author of guilt and ruin to his posterity; the latter, as the author of righteousness, life and salvation to those who are interested in him, by his obedience, atonement, and all powerful grace: And that he is so described, as the Antetype of Adam; sustaining, in that character, the office of mediator between God and man.[27]

The atonement was therefore central to Christ's identity and role as the second Adam. The dual headship of these two Adams would become the principal, overarching framework for Furman's entire biblical theology. Furman broadly conceived of salvation history as the two-act drama between two "public heads of mankind." With Adam as the "author of guilt" and Christ as the "author of righteousness," the Furmanian atonement was thus a recovery of fallen mankind in salvation through Christ's obedience. Ultimately, Furman understood Christ more as representative than as substitute.

Nevertheless, Furman did not view the two Adams of history in absolutely symmetrical terms. There is a universality in Adam that does not correspond in Christ. While Adam was the "head" of the entire fallen world, Christ cannot be said to represent the entire world. His mediation is only on behalf of the elect. Furman urged that Christ's atonement was only valid for "those who are interested in him," not the entire world. Therefore, the whole of Adam's "posterity" is not necessarily represented in Christ's atonement. Furman called Jesus Christ the "Antetype of Adam," and then explained,

> [1st.] That the merit and grace of the Redeemer are represented as superabounding, beyond the guilt and direful consequences of Adam's Sin; so as to insure complete salvation to the persons interested in that grace; however they may be chargeable with many actual transgressions, in addition to their original guilt and depravity.
>
> 2d. The Apostle employs the same terms in designating, or describing the persons affected, or concerned in these transactions: Either as connected with Adam, and involved in his guilt and ruin; or with Jesus Christ, as the objects of his mediation. And this remark applies with equal force to the original greek, as to our English translation of the passage.[28]

Interesting to note here is Furman's language of "transactions." While Furman shied away from commercial themes, this term is fundamentally linked

---

27. Furman, "Of Infant Salvation," 592.
28. Furman, "Of Infant Salvation," 592.

to his doctrine of the atonement and specifically to his doctrine of imputation. For Furman, in addition to their own personal transgressions, sinners possess "original guilt and depravity" by virtue of receiving Adam's sin and guilt in a kind of transfer. Likewise, Furman affirmed that the "objects" of Christ's mediation take part in a similar transaction whereby Christ's "merit" and "grace" become theirs by faith. Christ is more than their "head." His mediatorial work is fundamentally a "transaction" in which, similar to Adam, merits/demerits and righteousness/unrighteousness are issued.

According to Furman, Christ's obedience to the law in the Gospel was agreed upon between the Father and Son before the foundation of the world in a covenant called the covenant of redemption. In this eternal, intra-Trinitarian compact, the Father and Son agreed to procure a chosen people found in Christ. The result is a covenant of grace whereby Christ saves a people that cannot save themselves and becomes the head of a new humanity. Chapter 7.3 of *The Charleston Confession* states,

> This covenant is revealed in the gospel; first of all to Adam in the promise of salvation by the seed of the woman, and afterwards by farther steps, until the full discovery thereof was completed in the New Testament; and it is founded in that eternal covenant transaction that was been the Father and the Son about the redemption of the elect; and it is alone by the grace of this covenant that all of the posterity of fallen Adam that ever were saved did obtain life and blessed immortality, man now being utterly incapable of acceptance with God upon those terms on which Adam stood in his state of innocency.[29]

In this eternal agreement between the Father and Son, the intent, extent and nature of the atonement were set forth in Trinitarian counsel. This covenant also supplied the terms of Furman's doctrine of atonement. In a sermon entitled "The Constitution and Order of the Christian Church," Furman explained the unique identity of the church in terms of the covenant of redemption: "As his body, it is united to him by a threefold band of union: a federal, or covenant union, by his espousing their cause in the covenant of redemption; a natural union, by his assuming human nature; and a vital, or spiritual union, by giving them his spirit, and afford them life."[30] These three axioms each informed the way that Furman understood the nature of the atonement: federal, natural, and spiritual. By the incarnation, Jesus Christ wedded himself with humanity so that he could become the federal head of a new people indwelled with his Spirit. According to Furman, the headship of

29. *Charleston Confession of Faith*, 7.3.
30. Furman, "Constitution and Order of the Christian Church," 262.

Christ over his church is a federal, natural, and spiritual union, designed as such in the covenant of redemption. In a sermon delivered in 1802 entitled "Saints in Heavenly Rest," Furman explained the idea of union with Christ,

> First, union with him. Christ the Son of God has united his divinity to our nature by the assumption of a true body and rational soul; but believers are particularly and personally united to him by his Spirit, who dwells in their hearts. In consequence of their being so united to Christ, they partake of all the benefits of his mediation; his atonement, justifying righteousness; victory over the powers of hell, sin, and death; his intercession with the father; and, in a word, all the blessings of the new covenant. Believers are as really and intimately united to Christ, as the members of a body are to its head, and as branches, to the vine. And so necessary is their spiritual union with him, that without it our salvation is impossible.[31]

The doctrine of union with Christ was the vehicle by which Furman understood the blessings of the new covenant and the atonement which are delivered to believers. As David and Jonathan Gibson explained, the concept of union also furnishes an important distinction between a penal substitute and a representative penal substitute: "Union with Christ also defines the 'some' for whom his death is effective. It rescues us from an impoverished view of Christ's death as a mere 'instead of' penal substitutionary atonement for all, and instead presents us with a *representative* penal substitutionary atonement: Christ dies as *Someone* for *some* people."[32] Furman's covenantal framework supported a similar understanding of the atonement. Due to the representative nature of his doctrine of atonement, Furman remained within the bounds of a penal substitutionary model. However, representation and substitution are not identical concepts. Exactly how Furman distinguished them and remained inside a substitutionary frame will be discussed in the next chapter.

The atonement cannot be properly understood in Furman's system of thought without the covenant of redemption. Through the lens of this covenant, the atonement is God's loving action whereby the church is given and united to its bridegroom, the Son, in blood. For Furman, "God is a covenant God, and they are his covenant people."[33] Despite Furman's evangelical conviction that the gospel was intended for "men of all nations, ranks, characters, and capacities" and that "Gospel grace is of vast extent,"

---

31. Furman, "Saints in Heavenly Rest."
32. Gibson and Gibson, "Sacred Theology and the Reading of the Divine Word," 48.
33. Furman, "Children of Church Members," 490.

Furman's Two-Part Doctrine of Atonement   49

his overarching covenantal framework, anchored in the eternal covenant of redemption, dictated that Furman always adhered to some kind of limited understanding of the atonement.[34] For instance, while not explicitly outlining limited atonement in detail, Furman described the benefits of the atonement as reserved for the church. In his exegesis of Romans 4, Furman insisted, "This, St. Paul shows, is expressive of justification, and peace with God, through Christ's obedience, and propitiatory sacrifice: the benefits of which are applied to the souls of real penitents and believers. Their guilt, through his atonement, is completely removed; and, by the act of grace, cast, as it were, into the depths of the sea, to be seen or remembered no more."[35] Due to his understanding of application and the covenants, Furman's atonement language is mostly universal in nature but also limited in some way. In his sermon on infant salvation, Furman discussed "their receiving an application of the Savior's benefits" and "applying to them the blessings of his obedience, atonement, intercession and renewing grace, to reconcile them to God." In other words, the atonement is for all but its benefits are only for the church. There are elements of limited and unlimited atonement. Furman's doctrine of election narrowed his view of the atonement's intent. Later in the circular letter, he grounded his belief in the universal salvation of infants in the decrees of God, explaining its compatibility with the Calvinistic doctrine of unconditional election:

> The scheme here adopted for explanation of the doctrine, which we think is the scriptural one, does not militate against the doctrine of original sin, human depravity, the necessity of regeneration, nor any other important doctrine of the gospel, as far as we can discern. It is not viewed by us as opposing the scriptural doctrine of election, and the divine decrees. If children, dying in infancy, are in the scriptures designated as subjects of grace and salvation; to believe, or to assert they are so, no more militates against the sovereign, discriminating grace of God, than to say, that of those who arrive at a state of rational maturity, believers and penitents, are such subjects: The salvation of the whole being ascribed to the Redeemer's merit and grace; and being considered as effectively ordered by the divine decree.[36]

Whereas Adam's transgression under the covenant of works brought death, God has now made another covenant with Christ, the second Adam, so that believers may be found righteous on the basis of Christ's

---

34. Furman, "Royal Marriage Feast," 472.
35. Furman, "Conversion Essential to Salvation," 433.
36. Furman, "Of Infant Salvation," 599.

righteousness under the same law. Whereas Adam was condemned, Christ is found blameless. By the "covenant of grace," salvation comes to the elect by being found in the one who has kept the law. On the basis of Christ's fulfillment of the law, God now makes a gracious covenant with believers in Christ wherein the second Adam now stands as their representative head. In this regard, Furman was consistent with 7.2 of the *Charleston Confession* which reads, "man having brought himself under the curse of the law by his fall, it pleased the Lord to make a covenant of grace, wherein he freely offereth unto sinners life and salvation by Jesus Christ, requiring of them faith in him, that they may be saved; and promising to give unto all those that are ordained unto eternal life, his Holy Spirit, to make them willing and able to believe."[37]

Furman understood this "covenant of grace" as encompassing both the Old Testament and the New Testament in the Scriptures. Citing Hebrews 8, Furman insists,

> the old and new covenant mean the former and present dispensations, which, according to the hypothesis we have laid down, are dispensations of the same covenant, to wit, the covenant of grace—The one being dark, shadowy, united with carnal ordinances, and administered in general to carnal subjects, is represented as become old and passing away—The other, declared to be not like the former, and established in the gospel church, is particularly distinguished in this, that it should be made with spiritual subjects, and that the evidence of their interest in, and right to this covenant, should be, not the sign of circumcision in their flesh, but the law of God, put and written in their hearts.[38]

In short, Furman believed that both the old and new covenants in Scripture were "dispensations" within the same covenant of grace. Even though every human being is subject to and condemned under the covenant of works in Adam, God's plan of redemption is already underway in the moments after Adam's sin. Therefore, God's covenant with Abraham is a "type" of the grander covenant of grace made with believers in Christ:

> For if we grant the covenant made with Abraham was the covenant of grace, it must also be granted by our opponents, that it was an imperfect dispensation of that covenant to which the gospel has succeeded.... The glorious dispensation of the gospel has for its archetype, or pattern, not the imperfect dispensation to Abraham and the Jewish church; but the covenant

---

37. *Charleston Confession of Faith*, 7.2.
38. Furman, "Children of Church Members," 490.

itself, as made with Christ; which is now more fully revealed, and enjoyed in a church state, and with ordinances, must better adapted to its spiritual nature and original grand design.[39]

Unlike his Presbyterian counterparts, Furman distinguished the people of God in the new covenant not in any kind of familial or blood relation, but strictly in terms of faith in Christ's gracious atonement. Therefore, in many ways, Furman's Baptist identity was founded upon his definition of the covenant of grace.

Tripartite Work of Christ

Inside of this covenantal matrix, Furman understood the atonement as the centerpiece and essence of Christ's work of redemption. In the covenant of grace, Furman viewed the work of Christ as essentially threefold: (1) righteous obedience, (2) atonement in blood, (3) and living intercession. These three touchstones form the bedrock of Furman's soteriology, and they each appear routinely in his writings. Speaking of the covenant of grace, Furman explained that Jesus Christ "has consummated the spiritual marriage with this church, by taking her into a special covenant relationship to him, as her Savior. Blessings of the most excellent kind on which souls may Feast, are provided. Here are pardon, justification, acceptance, and peace with God; through the Redeemer's meritorious obedience, atonement, and intercession."[40] This tripartite scheme is fundamental to Furman's doctrine of atonement. It was often accompanied by language of justification, pardon, and acceptance, all near-synonyms for their corresponding concepts of obedience, atonement, and intercession. In one way or another, Furman included this threefold order in almost all of his major writings. The life-death-life sequence is pervasive in both his sermons and letters.

In George Washington's funeral sermon, Furman urged his audience "to obtain an interest in the justifying righteousness, atoning blood, and living intercession of the adorable Redeemer, who is the resurrection and the life."[41] In some instances, Furman kept the same order of the tripartite scheme but changed the words slightly, as he did in the sermon entitled "On the Communion of Saints." In the sermon, Furman described Christ's salvation of sinners as "the blood, righteousness and intercession of the Divine Redeemer for pardon, justification and acceptance before God."[42] On other

---

39. Furman, "Children of Church Members," 489.
40. Furman, "Royal Marriage Feast," 468.
41. Furman, "Humble Submission to Divine Sovereignty," 385.
42. Furman, "On the Communion of Saints," 564. Furman usually did not include

occasions, Furman added a brief addendum regarding sanctification, but never without first adhering strictly to his familiar tripartite scheme, and not without a focus upon reconciliation as the heart of Christ's atonement. For example, Furman spoke of Christ "applying to them the blessings of his obedience, atonement, intercession, and renewing grace, to reconcile them to God."[43] So pervasive was this repetition within Furman's soteriological framework that his doctrine of atonement can hardly be understood apart from it.

In Furman's mind, sincere faith itself included a belief in this tripartite scheme. Furman asserted that faith "consists in a firm persuasion, on the testimony of heaven, that Jesus is the Son of God, and the only Savior of men; and in such a reliance on his justifying righteousness, atoning blood, and living intercession, as causes us to cleave to him as the anchor of our hope, the ark of our safety, and city of our refuge."[44] According to Richard Furman, the threefold work of Christ was not simply a theological fact; it was essential to salvation itself. A sinner clung to these three evangelical truths.

The correspondence between Christ's righteousness and justification, Christ's atonement and pardon, and Christ's intercession and the sinner's acceptance with God all further reveal the way that Furman conceived of these soteriological categories. As mentioned earlier, Furman was nearly incapable of even mentioning the idea of justification without Christ's righteousness. The two were inseparable concepts in his frame of mind. This same kind of connection is true of the atonement and pardon. As previously demonstrated, the idea of pardon is one Furman reserved specifically for the atonement itself. In fact, on some occasions, while mentioning Christ's righteousness and his intercession, Furman was willing to leave out the word atonement altogether in place of pardon or blood or both. For example, speaking of the covenant of grace in a circular letter, Furman espoused that "by the same covenant," God offered the sinner "pardon by his blood, justification by his righteousness, and access to God through his intercession."[45] In this instance, the word "blood" becomes a synecdoche for the atonement, revealing the cruicentric lens through which Furman viewed Christ's saving work. While Christ could be said to atone for sinners by his life and death, Furman viewed the principal part of the atonement in

---

the theme of resurrection in this tripartite scheme.

43. Furman, "Of Infant Salvation," 597.

44. Furman, "Sermon, Occasioned by the Death of the Honor Major General Alexander Hamilton," 236.

45. Furman, "On Growth in Grace," 554.

terms of Christ's sacrificial death. In his mind, if there was no blood, there was no atonement.

The concept of pardon serves as the bridge by which Richard Furman tethered his penal substitutionary view of the atonement with another pervasive theme in his writings: moral government. For Furman, God was not simply Creator and Judge of all the earth; he was also a majestic Governor who ruled the earth according to his manifold moral perfections. Furman's governmental view of God was so influential to his doctrine of atonement that he was even willing to refer to the atonement as "divine clemency."[46] Casting one's soul upon the blood of Christ was similar to appealing to the mercy of a benevolent Governor for leniency. This is a chief reason the word "pardon" is so tightly linked to the idea of atonement and the reason the act of pardon is the leading benefit of Christ's saving work in so many of Furman's writings. For Furman, the gospel "gives assurance of free pardon, acceptance, and salvation through him, a joyful sound."[47] As the essence of Christ's atonement, pardon encapsulated the moral, political, and judicial themes that Furman saw in the atonement itself. It also fit nicely into his evangelistic appeals. He once asked his audience,

> Have we awoke to the serious consideration of eternal things; to a discovery of our guilt and depravity, and of divine wrath as ready to overwhelm a guilty, impenitent world? Has divine mercy also appeared to us in the gospel, and Christ been endeared in all the amiableness of his character and sufficiency of grace? Have we, in the exercise of divine faith, fled for refuge to his mediation; do we trust in his immaculate righteousness for justification before God, and to his atoning blood for pardon?[48]

For Furman, grace wasn't simply a verdict delivered by a righteous and merciful Judge; it was also the forgiveness of a guilty sentence by the just Ruler and Governor of all the earth. There is no meaningful use of the term "pardon" without the idea of impending wrath. The sinner is effectively pardoned of their guilt on the basis of Christ's death, his passive obedience, in order to satisfy the wrath of the Father on their behalf.

Furman's emphasis upon pardon also stemmed from his view of public justice. Christ's atonement for the sins of the elect had implications for the pardoned sinner as well as for the honor of the pardoning Governor. Therefore, the atonement was the simultaneous display of retributive justice in the Lamb of God as penal substitute and of rectoral justice in Christ the

---

46. Furman, "Conversion Essential to Salvation," 433.
47. Furman, "Royal Marriage Feast," 470.
48. Furman, "Unity and Peace," 307.

penal example, vindicating the Lawgiver and Governor now glorified for his many moral perfections. By equating atonement with pardon, Furman tethered judicial and political themes that helped him to integrate penal substitutionary and moral governmental views of the atonement into the same soteriological framework. These will be explored in the next section.

Moral Governmental Atonement

In upholding a form of penal substitutionary atonement, Richard Furman viewed the death of Christ as the meting out of a punishment according to the penal demands of the law. In this two-way imputation, the sin and guilt of the elect are transferred to the crucified Christ, who gives his life for the church. Conversely, the righteous merits of Christ are also reckoned to the elect, who are accounted guiltless on the basis of Christ's righteous life through faith. For this reason, the concept of imputation is fundamental to Richard Furman's doctrine of the atonement. Furman understood imputation as just one part of an eternal covenant between the Father and the Son to procure an elect people to be united to the Son. However, for the moderate Calvinist Furman, the atonement was much more than simply about vicarious punishment or aversion of divine anger. For Furman, the atoning work of Christ could not be adequately described in merely judicial or even forensic terms. It was also deeply moral and governmental in nature.

Furman's friend and fellow Baptist Jonathan Maxcy adequately described the moral governmental view of the atonement when he posited, "The atonement made by Christ presented the law, the nature of sin, and the displeasure of God against it, in such a light, that no injury would accrue to the moral system, no imputations would be against the righteousness of the great Legislator, though he should forgive the sinner, and instate him in eternal felicity."[49] Jonathan Edwards Jr. outlined the moral governmental view, "The atonement is the substitute for the punishment threatened in the law and was designed to answer the same ends of supporting the authority of the law, the dignity of the divine moral government, and the consistency of the divine conduct in legislation and execution."[50] Richard Furman understood the atonement in similar terms. No matter the degree of mercy shown, no injury whatsoever could be done to "the great Legislator" or His law. In his forgiveness and lovingkindness, God must never be seen as less than completely just. The divine character and reputation are at

---

49. Maxcy, "Discourse Designed to Explain the Doctrine of the Atonement," 207. Maxcy originally delivered this sermon in 1796.

50. Edwards, "Necessity of Atonement," in Park, *Atonement*, 6.

stake. According to Furman, to break a law "when the necessity for it is so great and apparent, is, in effect, to charge the Great Moral Governor with having delivered a defective system."[51] The atonement is thus a restoration and a vindication of God's righteous rule in the most public way.[52] Daniel W. Cooley and Douglas A. Sweeney explained what they call the "New England moral government theory of the atonement" in these terms:

> The atonement is about restoring God's divine rule; man's redemption is a felicitous by-product of that restoration. The atonement is designed to vindicate the righteousness and justice of divine law. Vindication means that 'God is determined to support the authority of his law, and he will not suffer it to fall into contempt.' It means that God has shown and will show that he acts in accordance with divine law. This vindication is not merely a vindication of a set of statutes but of the very character of God. If God's law falls into disrepute, it is because God has failed to uphold it.[53]

Furman too was determined to show that Christ had honored the authority and justice of divine law by his sacrificial death. He also believed that this death was consistent with a completely free pardon of sinners, a signature part of the moral government scheme. "Because Christ does this," Oliver Crisp reasons, "God is able to forgive sinners. His moral governance is vindicated, and Christ's work generates a merit sufficient in principle for the salvation of all humanity."[54]

However, unlike Jonathan Maxcy, who became the first president of South Carolina College in 1804 in large part due to Furman's political influence, Furman himself did not believe that penal substitution and God's moral government were mutual exclusive concepts in the atonement. Furman actually employed the theme of moral government as consistently and relentlessly as Maxcy did. Although not rejecting it outright like Maxcy, Furman downplayed the idea that the atonement was the payment of a debt. In contrast to Calvinistic Baptist contemporaries in the South like Jesse Mercer (1769–1841), who explicitly affirmed the atonement as a debt payment, almost nowhere in Furman's writings can pecuniary language such as

---

51. Furman, "Richard Furman to Gabriel Gerald," Richard Furman Papers, Acc. 1960-016 [Box #1, Folder #11], Special Collections and Archives, Furman University, Greenville, S.C.

52. For an excellent treatment of the Edwardsean moral governmental view, see Rudisill, *Doctrine of the Atonement in Jonathan Edwards and His Successors*, 83–112.

53. Cooley and Sweeney, "Edwardseans and the Atonement," 120–21.

54. Crisp, "Moral Government of God," 87.

"purchase" be found, other than in citations of Scripture.⁵⁵ For Furman, the atonement was about pardon and not about payment.

In this moral governmental scheme, forgiveness is not a debt paid but a divine legal acquittal that a sinner receives by faith. However, in this merciful acquittal, absolutely nothing can impugn the righteousness of God in judgment. Furman's doctrine of atonement was far more about paying honor to the Lawgiver than paying the debt of the sinner. Therefore, the Furmanian atonement becomes fundamentally about honoring divine justice in the act of exoneration. Furman was not afraid to describe the atonement as "divine clemency."

The idea of pardon fit nicely into Furman's governmental framework. In vindicating the authority and justice of God, the atonement is designed to emphasize the free grace and moral excellence of the moral governor of all the earth. For Furman, this divine pardon was not a flippant act by a capricious governor. Instead, it was performed according to the careful terms of God's law, upholding and displaying its moral rigor and indelible character. The atonement secures the conditions for pardon so that sin is shown to be infinitely evil and God is shown to be infinitely just. In his treatment of moral governmental theory amongst New Divinity revivalists, Robert W. Caldwell III explains, "As God's moral attributes are discerned, known, and loved in creation, the universe increasingly shines with the reflected glory of God. Today evangelicals might call this manifestation of God in history the 'kingdom of God'; the New Divinity preferred to call it God's moral government."⁵⁶ As Furman was influenced by this group of theologians, of whom Maxcy himself was a part, the South Carolinian spoke in New Divinity terms. Therefore, when speaking of the atonement, Furman often blended retributive justice and rectoral justice, viewing the atonement in both personal and public terms. As the second Adam, Jesus Christ is the savior, substitute, and representative of the elect. However, he fulfills none of these roles without vindicating the moral attributes of the moral governor simultaneously.

In order to understand Furman's view of the atonement, the concept of God's moral perfections is critical because of the way that Furman viewed the publicity of the atonement. Christ's atoning work is designed by God to be seen and adored by a worshipping audience. It is a public event meant to display what God has done as well as his character and his nature. In

---

55. See Mercer, *Ten Letters, Addressed to the Reverend Cyrus White, in reference to his Scriptural view of the Atonement*, 7–10.

56. Caldwell, *Theologies of the American Revivalists*, 94.

a hymn that he composed for the twenty-sixth anniversary of American Independence, Furman wrote a doxology in terms of salvation "displayed":

> He saved us in the hour
> When huge affliction rose;
> For us displayed delivering power,
> And triumphed over our foes![57]

Furman interpreted God's salvation as an exhibition of divinity. In saving sinners (in this case the American people), God "displayed delivering power." Like so many Puritan descendants, Furman's American sense of destiny and deliverance was often expressed in messianic terms. Similar to the people of Israel witnessing the great power of the Lord against the Egyptians (Exod 14:30–31), Furman viewed both the salvation of Americans from British tyranny as well as salvation from sin as displays of God's powerful nature. Thus, Furman believed that the atonement was public because it was ultimately designed to display God.

In the moral governmental scheme, God's attributes deserve acknowledgement. Furman extolled the "Creator of the world, having completed a glorious and harmonious system of nature by his power, wisdom, and goodness—As the independent and eternal Sovereign, asserting his natural and moral Government over his creation, and demanding their acknowledgement and allegiance."[58] God saves sinners to display himself, but not just one part of himself. For Furman, God's government is upheld by every single one of his moral attributes, thus the term "moral government" is one that Furman employs frequently in his writings. Richard Furman believed that the telos of the incarnation, atonement, and resurrection was to display the divine moral perfections. Even human sin was ordained for this specific purpose. In a 1798 circular letter entitled "On the Use of Reason in Religion," Furman insisted, "For the incarnation, obedience, and sufferings of the Son of God; man's depravity and guilt, God's strict justice on the one hand, and his design of showing mercy, in a manner consistent with his glorious perfections and righteous government, on the other, are assigned as reasons."[59] Furman's equivalence with "glorious perfections" and "righteous government" is indicative of the way he viewed God's moral government. In short, God's government of the earth is designed to display His multifaceted glory. Furman shared this view with other southern Baptist adherents

---

57. Furman, "America's Deliverance and Duty," 410.

58. Furman, "Richard Furman to Gabriel Gerald," Richard Furman Papers, Acc. 1960-016 [Box #1, Folder #11], Special Collections and Archives, Furman University, Greenville, S.C.

59. Furman, "On the Use of Reason in Religion," 529.

of moral government, including William B. Johnson, who insisted that the grand plan of "the great moral Governor of the Universe" is to display his "natural and moral attributes" to moral believers.[60]

Therefore, when Furman addresses the topic of God's government, he almost always includes language of perfections, glory, and attributes. Furman believed this was consistent with biblical revelation and human reason. He concluded, "Exhortations, commands, promises, invitations, and threatenings, are enforced by arguments, taken from the perfections and government of the Deity."[61] Even the particular way that God communicated himself to and dealt with humanity served to display his perfections and government upon the earth. The divine government is not simply a soteriological category, but also a creational one. Both God's providence over the earth and his salvation of sinners both attested to the same moral government. "The government of the world by divine providence," wrote Furman, "is a truth evinced both by reason and revelation, and has been exemplified in the history of all nations, in every age and every clime."[62]

Furman held to the idea that the chief goal of the gospel was to extol the moral government of God. The vindication of the divine government is the supreme, crowning effect of the good news of Christ. In some instances, Furman would even frame the gospel in explicit terms of moral government. For example, Furman once averred that God's grace was to "corroborate the design of his gospel, and promote the interest of his moral government."[63] Both providence and salvation served to promote the moral perfections of God for his glory. Even when Furman detailed the manifold blessings of the believer in salvation, these blessings are all subsumed under the idea of God's glory displayed. Furman treated God's moral government as the "crown" of the entire gospel scheme itself. In his sermon entitled "Unity and Peace," Furman boasted,

> To counteract so great an evil, to prevent the exercise of base passions, to restore lost man an acquaintance with his true interests, and to furnish an example of disinterested, generous love; the peaceable kingdom of Christ has been erected. In accomplishing these great purposes also, the malice and artifice of hell are overthrown, immortal souls are rescued out of the hands of the enemy, united in a fraternal band here, and prepared for a future state of most refined society and everlasting bliss: and,

---

60. Johnson, "Love Characteristic of the Deity," 42.
61. Furman, "On the Use of Reason in Religion," 529.
62. Furman, "Oration, Delivered at the Charleston Orphan-House," 349.
63. Furman, "Oration, Delivered at the Charleston Orphan-House," 349.

to crown the whole, the most illustrious display of the moral perfections of the Deity, is given in their salvation. What are all the boasts victories of heroes—what are the boasted improvements of legislators, statesmen, or philosophers, compared with this triumph of the Redeemer in establishing his kingdom of peace?[64]

Excerpts such as these prove that Furman was prone on occasion to view God's moral government and his kingdom as near-synonyms. The establishment of God's "kingdom of peace" is simultaneously the "most illustrious display of the moral perfections of the Deity" given in the salvation of the elect. Furman preferred kingly language as well as legislative language to describe God's government upon the earth. In a letter to Oliver Hart, Furman confessed,

> It is a comfortable consideration that the influences of Divine Grace are so abundantly diffused to the Northward. O that the Redeemer's Kingdom may be extended far and wide, till the whole Earth may own his Government, and the radiant beams of Divine Truth dispel the clouds of moral and spiritual darkness which have so long overspread the face of things.[65]

The subject of God's moral government was of such importance for Richard Furman that its significance could be seen in countless other doctrines, including infant baptism. Speaking on the sensitive topic of deceased children, Furman found the doctrine of divine moral government to be relevant. He insisted, "To pious, benevolent minds, of extended views, the subject acquires additional importance when viewed in connection with the Moral Government of the deity, and with the riches and glory of that grace which is displayed in Salvation by Jesus Christ."[66] For this sensitive and highly controversial subject, Furman not only associated God's moral government with the gospel itself; he also believed that it actually provided "additional importance" to the issue of infant salvation. God's moral government was of such vast significance in the thinking of Richard Furman that it could not be outweighed by something as compelling as the subject of the eternal fate of children. As a result, it surfaces frequently in his writings on the atonement. Not even the resurrection could escape its significance.

---

64. Furman, "Unity and Peace," 302.

65. Furman, "Richard Furman to Oliver Hart," Richard Furman Papers, Acc. 1960-016 [Box #1, Folder #1], Special Collections and Archives, Furman University, Greenville, S.C.

66. Furman, "Of Infant Salvation," 586.

Furman insisted that "Christ's mediation and honor of God's moral government are concerned in the event."[67]

Honor

If Richard Furman publicized the atonement, nothing was more essential to his idea of publicity than the concept of honor. As a public reward, honor greatly supported his moral governmental theory of the atonement. By publicly vindicating the justice of the divine Lawgiver, Christ's atonement was an honoring of God. In other words, Christ's death displayed God's moral attributes to his creation. For Furman, when God or humanity is shown to be morally right, they are awarded with honor. For this reason, Furman believed that someone who exercised Christian love also exhibited a "due regard to the honor of God."[68] To seek one's happiness and to seek the honor of God, in Furman's mind, were not mutually exclusive desires. For instance, in the circular letter entitled "On the Use of Reason in Religion," Furman encouraged his audience to "act up to the dignity of your nature; as a rational creature, concerned for your own true happiness; for the honor of God, as his servant; and for the welfare of mankind, as a friend and brother of the great human family."[69] Both individual happiness and the welfare of the world were found in the honoring of the Creator and Moral Governor of the world.

When God pardons sinners in Christ, he does so in a way that displays his glorious perfections and honors himself as Moral Governor. This includes both his righteous love for what is good and his righteous displeasure for evil. Both of these are on display in the atonement. Christ's righteous obedience under the law and his satisfaction of the law's righteous demands are both consistent with the righteousness of God, exhibiting his love for what is good (i.e., justice) and his hatred for what is bad (i.e., sin). In a circular letter entitled "On the Languishing State of Religion in the Southern States" penned in 1799, Furman described the sin of professing believers in terms of God's honor and His displeasure toward sin:

> Let us ask: Is this honoring God with the best of our substance and service? If the man who neglects to provide according to his ability, for the support of needy relatives, has, in the judgment of an inspired apostle, denied the faith and is worse than an infidel;

---

67. Furman, "Of Infant Salvation," 593.
68. Furman, "Unity and Peace," 302.
69. Furman, "On the Use of Reason in Religion," 527.

what shall we say of those who are thus neglectful of the church and cause of God?—Shall these evils exist, indulged, among a professing people, whose obligations exceed all that an angel can conceive, or everlasting returns of gratitude discharge, and yet not be marked with tokens of divine displeasure on the authors of them, by him who has made himself known as a holy God, jealous of his honor?—Certainly not![70]

In short, because God is "jealous of his honor," sin cannot be left unpunished, otherwise, as the Moral Governor of the universe, God would be seen as unjust and ultimately dishonorable. The honor of God is the ethical foundation for the moral governmental theory of the atonement. For God to show mercy upon sinners in a way inconsistent with his own law is to impugn his righteousness and to bring dishonor upon himself as an immoral Legislator. Therefore, for Furman, any seemingly moral act that is inconsistent with God's justice is dishonorable and thus sinful.

Furman's doctrine of sin was equally public. Sin and dishonor were near-synonyms in Furman's mind. According to Furman, sin is dishonorable both for its inherent evil as well as for its public promotion of evil. Furman explained that covetousness "not only dishonors God by the evil contained in itself, but by opening the door to many other great evils, and thereby increasing, beyond what we can readily conceive, the sum or measure of human guilt and pollution in the world."[71] Furman then addressed the nature of sin, making a distinction between its private and public components:

> In private life, what frauds, exactions, and extortions are produced by it! To the oppression of the poor, or servants, and dependents—To the distress of the fatherless and widows—To the injury of neighbors, friends and relatives—and to the grief of God's Church. In public life, how often does it pollute the fountain of law and justice, by bribery and corruption! How does it prompt men, by a thousand arts to seek and hold stations of authority and power, only as they are the means of obtaining wealth and consequence![72]

The inherent, "private" evil of sin is the reason it must be punished and reparations made. However, the "public" element of sin is the reason that the Father's righteousness must be publicly vindicated because the Moral Governor must be honored. Justice must be satisfied for honor's sake. In Furman's words, sin can "pollute the fountain of law and justice," making a

---

70. Furman, "On the Languishing State of Religion in the Southern States," 536.
71. Furman, "On Covetousness," 578.
72. Furman, "On Covetousness," 578.

mockery of the Lawgiver. As a result, the atonement is intimately connected to the moral government of God. Open transgression demands a lawful response from the Legislator. In response to the public evil of sin, the atonement publicly honors God as the supreme moral Being and Rector whose divine displeasure for sin will never be questioned. Jesus defeats sin and puts the powers of evil to open shame by pardoning sin with his own blood.

In this same vein, Furman interpreted faith in terms of giving honor to God. For example, for a sinner to break God's law is to "not be concerned for the honor of God."[73] However, according to Furman, repentance is a "sorrow for having offended and dishonored the Most High."[74] In his sermon entitled "On the Constitution and Order of the Christian Church" preached in 1790, Furman distinguished true believers as those who exercise "supreme love to God; subjection to his authority and government; a zealous concern for the honor of the divine majesty; an open profession of his name; and an unshaken attachment to his cause, interest and people."[75] So enraptured was Furman with the thought of receiving the "privilege" of salvation that he exclaimed, "How sublime the honor! every humble believer who pursues the interest of that kingdom, shares."[76] The atonement vindicated the public honor of the Moral Governor while also bestowing personal honor to every believer found in Christ, their personal substitute and representative. The combination of these two themes is where Richard Furman found legitimate grounds for integrating both penal substitutionary and moral governmental views of the atonement. In the Furmanian atonement, the public and private spheres unite in the honorable pardoning of sinners.

In this way, the gospel is an honoring of both God and man in the atonement. Therefore, to abide in the covenant of grace is to walk in the appointed means of grace, which Furman defined in terms of honor: "Be serious, regular, and fervent in prayer; and in the use of all the appointed means of grace, whether of a more common or special nature. Cherish the most pure and generous sentiments towards your fellow-creatures; and exercise a holy zeal for the honor of your God."[77] In light of his grace, to worship God is essentially to honor God as Lawgiver and as Moral Governor.

---

73. Furman, "Children of Church Members," 488.
74. Furman, "Royal Marriage Feast," 469.
75. Furman, "Constitution and Order," 260.
76. Furman, "Unity and Peace," 305.
77. Furman, "On Growth in Grace," 555.

4

A Systematic Theological Treatment of Furman's Doctrine of Atonement

Satisfaction: Legal vs. Commercial

UPHOLDING DIVINE JUSTICE AND the goodness of the law was a hallmark of the New Divinity, an American school of theology which Furman closely mirrored at times. In fact, legal language pervaded their entire system of thinking. According to Peter Jauhiainen, "Constitutional language also shaped the New Divinity's governmental theory of the atonement, one of its more significant departures from traditional Calvinism. It replaced a limited substitutionary model wherein Christ paid a debt for the elect with an unlimited one that emphasized the role of Christ's death in upholding the authority of divine law."[1] According to the theological scheme of many of Jonathan Edwards's disciples, the purpose of the atonement was the satisfaction of divine justice, not the payment of a literal price.[2] As a result, New Divinity men were often hesitant to use commercial or pecuniary language to describe the atonement, instead using legal vocabulary. Richard Furman exhibited the same tendency. However, true to his eclectic style, he did not do so completely. Furman was not a thoroughgoing New Divinity man.

Richard Furman consistently emphasized the natural guilt of his hearers along with the inherent goodness of the law. In his eulogy of Baptist John

1. Jauhiainen, "Samuel Hopkins and Hopkinsianism," 116.

2. Many of these Edwardsean theologians emphasized the law because they believed themselves to be preaching to a hyper-capitalistic culture of ambition, avarice, and dissolution Charles Sellers has even identified this Edwardsean aversion to American greed as part of "the New Divinity's anticapitalist polemic" (Sellers, *Market Revolution*, 206).

Gano, Furman praised his friend's homiletics and his right use of the law: "he asserted and maintained the honor of his God, explained the meaning of the Divine Law,—showing its purity and justice,—exposed the sinner's guilt—proved him to be miserable, ruined and inexcusable, and called him in unfeigned, immediate repentance."[3] In a Pauline sense, Furman insisted that it was the sinner who was defiled and not the law. The latter was, in some ways, an embodiment of the good and just character of God. Therefore, the claims of justice in the law only supported the good government of God. Divine goodness and divine justice did not necessarily rest in opposite corners in Richard Furman's theology.

So important was the law in Furman's soteriology that he often ascribed divine characteristics to the law and justice anthropomorphically, as he would have to God himself. In a circular letter entitled "On the Use of Reason in Religion," Furman explained that God's illuminating grace shows sinners "the divine goodness and sovereignty, the righteousness and spirituality of God's law."[4] Similarly, on multiple occasions Furman opined about the "rights of justice, and the principles of humanity" and the sins that "infringe the rights of justice, and are highly offensive to God."[5] In some ways, Furman believed that justice was more than simply an attribute of God; it had its own "rights." Like any others, these rights were to be defended. To speak of the law was virtually to speak of God himself. For Furman, the law exposed the heinous nature of sin and revealed its just deserts. In doing so, it declared the moral goodness of God. In turn, the law became for Furman a centerpiece of the atonement whereby Christ endured the curse of the law in order to pardon sinners while also living a life of lawfulness to impute to their account. Consequently, God is both just and justifier of the ungodly, Moral Governor and Pardoner of the elect. The atonement is a vindication of the honor of God, the "rights" of justice, and the righteousness of the law.

However, Furman did not confuse the roles of law and gospel in the salvation of sinners. He did not preach a message of works righteousness. In a sermon preached before the Charleston Association in 1790 entitled "On the Constitution and Order of the Christian Church," Furman delivered one of his most detailed presentations of the gospel scheme, clearly explaining the ultimate relationship between law and grace. He exhorted his fellow Baptist ministers to preach in a way that displayed the enormity of Christ's person and work. The result was one of the most compelling examples of Furmanian homiletics:

---

3. Cited in Baker and Craven, *Adventure in Faith*, 197.
4. Furman, "On the Use of Right Religion," 524.
5. Furman, "Of Covetousness," 578; Furman, "On Growth in Grace," 558.

> Here again he must distinguish between the law and gospel; and between the characters of men, as saints and sinners: Must point out the ruined and guilty state of all, by nature, under the curse of a broken law; sound, as it were, Mount Sinai's thunder in the sinner's ear; present the flaming mountain to his eye; and thus produce the awful evidence, to that momentous truth, "that by the deeds of the law, shall no flesh living be justified." To the humbled sinner, and believing soul, he must describe Jesus, as "the Lamb of God, who taketh away the sins of the world." As the only, the almighty, and the willing savior. He must describe him, in his person, his offices, his works of love and grace, his bleeding passion, and triumphant state. He must open, as it were, Immanuel's heart, in the description of divine compassion, and publish the gracious invitation of the gospel, to perishing and heavy-laden souls; must shew the abundant grace contained in the promises, and the foundation on which faith may rest, in the faithfulness, infinite goodness, sovereign mercy, and unchangeable purpose of the promiser.[6]

Richard Furman's governmental substitutionary view of the atonement made it virtually impossible for him to describe the work of Christ without also presenting the goodness, divinity, and right use of the law. In the same letter to Gabriel Gerald, Furman wrote of the law's "just and benevolent design" and then explained that to break a law, "when the necessity for it is so great and apparent, is, in effect, to charge the Great Moral Governor with having delivered a defective system."[7] Furman's understanding of God's moral government hinged on the law and specifically its honor. In the law are displayed all the moral attributes of God, and to follow the law is to honor God in those attributes. Law-abiding Christians give expression to the perfections of God. Furman defined the moral law as "a rule of duty, given to intelligent creatures, which bears strict conformity to the moral perfections of God, and being founded in the highest reason, in respect to the divine perfections, the nature of the creatures, their relation to the Creator, and their obligations to him, is unchangeable and perpetual." Furman then insisted, "the distinction between moral and positive law is a distinction of modern theology."[8] In other words, God's law is not temporary. It is everlasting. Therefore, human laws should reflect divine law and should

---

6. Furman, "Constitution and Order," 274–75.

7. Furman, "Richard Furman to Gabriel Gerald," Richard Furman Papers, Acc. 1960-016 [Box #1, Folder #11], Special Collections and Archives, Furman University, Greenville, S.C.

8. Furman, "Richard Furman to Gabriel Gerald."

not be treated as something altogether separate from the character of God. Positivism had no place in the theology of Richard Furman.

The de-commercialized language of the New Divinity in describing the atonement was especially prominent among American Baptists. In Georgia, Jesse Mercer defended a form of moral governmental theory similar to Andrew Fuller. Mercer wrote,

> I do not mean to contend for the atonement, as a commercial transaction: but I mean to oppose the idea of a vague atonement. I must contend with Fuller that though we cannot view the great work of redemption as a commercial transaction betwixt a debtor and his creditor: yet the satisfaction of justice, in all cases, requires to be *equal* to what the nature of the offense is in reality—and to answer the *same end* as if the guilty party had actually suffered. And for Christ, as our substitute, to have suffered *less* for us than we should if the law had taken its course, would be no atonement at all, and leave us in our sins.[9]

Years after Furman's death, in *The Atonement of Christ*, James Madison Pendleton exhibited the same suspicion of commercial tropes as Fuller. Pendleton wrote, "The atonement has been often represented as a commercial transaction, proceeding on the principle of creditor and debtor, requiring so much suffering on the part of the Atoner for the salvation of so many." Representing well the views of many Baptists in the early nineteenth century on the atonement, Pendleton then warned,

> Thus a great moral transaction, worthy of God and in the highest sense, illustrative of his glory, is looked upon as the literal payment of a debt. Analogies, like figures of speech, must not be pressed too far. Sin can be regarded as a *debt* in a metaphorical sense only. A debt is something which one person owes to another; something due from one to another. It is plain in this sense sin is not a debt; for it is not what the creature *owes* the Creator, but the very opposite. Sin, however, exposes the sinner to the penalty of the divine law, of which it is the transgression. This exposure involves obligation to suffer the penalty. The endurance of the penalty is *due* from the transgressor. Sin, therefore, can only be termed a *debt* by that figure of speech which puts the cause for the effect, and the effect for the cause. As the effect of sin, the sinner may be said to owe a debt to the

---

9. Mercer, in Mallary, *Memoirs of Elder Jesse Mercer*, 290–91.

violated justice of God; but sin itself cannot be a literal debt. It is a crime.[10]

Such a de-commercialized doctrine of atonement was common among Baptists in Furman's day, and it signaled Andrew Fuller's influence upon American Baptist theology. Furman adhered to this kind of thinking. He was not fond of describing Christ's work in terms of value, worth, or any kind of amount which could enumerate the sufferings of Christ on a gradated scale. In fact, Furman almost never spoke of the atonement in commercial or pecuniary terms. However, in distinction from the New Divinity's de-commercialized doctrine of atonement, Furman's view can be more aptly described as an *un*-commercialized atonement. He did not do away with pecuniary language altogether. Sometimes he integrated both pecuniary and legal language in the same address. Furman once wrote a friend, critiquing his presentation of the atonement. Furman warned that his friend

> would incline persons, who do not know you, to think you favored Socinian, or legal principles in Divinity, by the representation it makes of Christ's work as being separate from the interests of his people, thought I am sure this was not your intention. But certain it is, though Christ wrought out the work of redemption alone, he representatively, and virtually, comprehended his people therein, and they may be said to have given satisfaction to justice by the obedience and sufferings he rendered as their surety. In him, also, they have obtained victory over their spiritual enemies, with him they have risen from the dead and are ascended to the triumphant state of bliss.[11]

Furman's use of the word "surety," or the responsibility taken for payment of a debt, is particularly interesting. Not only is this one of Furman's only documented uses of monetary language to describe the atonement; it is also utilized next to the language of legal satisfaction. The latter is a perfect example of how Furman did not necessarily see the two at odds, though he clearly preferred the language of satisfaction of divine justice.

Chapter 8.6 of the *Confession* addresses the "price of redemption" that was "paid by Christ."[12] Hence, in at least a minimal confessional sense, Fur-

---

10. Pendleton, *Atonement of Christ*, 88–89. This work was published when Pendleton was a pastor in Pennsylvania, but Pendleton's views do not suggest a significant change over time.

11. Furman, "Richard Furman to Gabriel Gerald," Richard Furman Papers, Acc. 1960–016 [Box #1, Folder #11], Special Collections and Archives, Furman University, Greenville, SC.

12. *Charleston Confession of Faith*, 8.6.

man did affirm some kind of payment of a moral debt in Christ's atonement. For instance, in one of the hymns that he composed, Furman spoke of the church as "Ye ransom'd people."[13] Therefore, Richard Furman's view of the atonement can be described as a moral governmental, un-commercialized atonement. Whereas many adamantly refused to employ the language of commercial or pecuniary transactions, Furman was sometimes willing to do so in order to explain the assurance a believer has in Christ.

Justice: Retributive vs. Rectoral

While Richard Furman clearly affirmed a doctrine of atonement that emphasized the satisfaction of divine justice, his specific view of justice was a theological blend. Although he did not use such explicit terms, Furman's dedication to the theme of moral government combined with his penal substitutionary frame ensured that he deployed both retributive and rectoral justice, while punctuating the latter. Retributive justice concerns the punishment of sinners and giving them their personal deserts. Rectoral justice concerns God's right governing of the universe. Furman was not the only theologian to attempt to blend these two styles of justice. In his article "Re-thinking Atonement in Jonathan Edwards and New England Theology," S. Mark Hamilton critiqued the Edwardsean combination of these two themes. Hamilton observed,

> It is interesting for our understanding of Edwards Sr. that his successors say so much of the rectoral demands of the moral law and so little, if anything, of the rectoral demands of God himself. This is perhaps telling of how we make sense of anomalous appearance of both substitutionary language, moral government language, and the oddities of Edwards' account of rectoral and retributive justice.[14]

Richard Furman's project was very similar, although perhaps not with the level of systematic treatment as that of Edwards. With a commitment to a penal substitutionary frame, Furman also relentlessly stressed the importance of honoring the Moral Governor in all things. As a result, rectoral justice took precedence in his thinking. The honor, authority, and integrity of the Moral Governor were paramount in his theology. As a result, Furman's doctrine of creation was largely informed by rectoral justice. Furman praised

---

13. Furman, "Hymn II," 410.

14. Hamilton, "Re-thinking Atonement in Jonathan Edwards and New England Theology," 98.

the "Creator of the world, having completed a glorious and harmonious system of nature by his power, wisdom, and goodness. As the independent and eternal Sovereign, [he] asserts his natural and moral government over his creation, and demands their acknowledgement and allegiance."[15] From the beginning, God established his creation in such a way that its administration would reflect upon the divine attributes, most especially God's moral attributes. The universe is an ethical exhibition. In fact, Furman believed that the "end of the gospel ministry" is to display the glory of God.[16] When divine image-bearers reflect upon the beauty of nature and the care which God exerts upon his creatures, they behold his goodness and his justice. In Furman's mind, this beholding is part of an intricate system designed to display the character of God. "Redemption," Furman contended, "in the moral system, appears to be the most glorious work of God."[17] Therefore justice isn't simply about meting out punishment upon sinners; it is a public relations matter for the King of the cosmos. God must always be seen as just and good and holy and righteous.

Whereas some, including Hamilton, might see these two types of justice at odds, Furman did not. In fact, in the very same sermon on Ps 39:4, Furman spoke of the "awful realities and righteous retribution" of God as well as the "transactions of judgment" which are "necessary for the honor of the divine government."[18] In hell, there is both retributive and rectoral justice. In a sermon preached after the death of Oliver Hart, Furman warned his hearers of "the great day of final retribution."[19] Furman viewed the punishment of the law as both the personal penalty due to sinners as well as something which expressed the integrity of the Lawgiver.

Richard Furman believed that the "genius" of the gospel was found in its accordance with the "laws of God."[20] These laws exacted a punishment while also exhibiting the character of God. In Furman's view, there was no contradiction between rectoral and retributive justice, between punishment of sin by a Ruler in order to uphold the consistency of his moral government and punishment of sin by a holy God in order to deal with the intrinsic evil of sin.[21] Justice is public because of the reputation of the Lawgiver and

15. Furman, "Richard Furman to Gabriel Gerald."
16. Furman, "Constitution and Order," 277.
17. Furman, "Richard Furman to Gabriel Gerald."
18. Richard Furman, Manuscript, sermon on Death, Psalm 39:4, undated, Richard Furman Papers, Acc. 1960–016 [Series II, Box #3, #3], Special Collections and Archives, Furman University, Greenville, SC.
19. Furman, "Rewards of Grace," 341.
20. Furman, "Unity and Peace," 303.
21. In his discussion of the Grotian governmental theory of the atonement, Oliver

"private" in the sense that an individual must receive what they personally deserve. Both satisfied divine justice in Furman's mind, but from seemingly different sides of the anthropological-theological divide. This coalescing of rectoral and retributive justice became one of the hallmarks of the Furmanian atonement.

In his sermon on Ps 89:48 ("What man is he that liveth, and shall not see death? Shall he deliver his soul from the hand of the grave?"), Furman spoke of sin both as an infraction of divine justice and as an evil deserving of punishment. He reasoned, "If the designs of mercy, for their accomplishment, require the removal of the righteous from their present state of existence as the claims of justice demand, no less, the death of the wicked: That they may cease to abuse the bounties of Providence, the divine long-suffering, and the day of grace; and suffer the infliction of that punishment which their sins deserve."[22] In this excerpt, Furman demonstrates a public understanding of justice in his view of the "claims of justice" and the "abuse" of the grace of God. In response to the transgression of sin, the law cannot be relaxed; instead there is a legal "demand." In other words, it is a necessity of justice that satisfaction be made for sin. However, Furman also adds that there is a "punishment which their sins deserve," indicating that God's wrath must be meted out in some way upon the sin itself. By virtue of God's righteous law, sin demands both rectoral justice and retributive justice. The Lawgiver must be vindicated because of who he is and sin must be addressed because of what it is. There is a penalty "due to sin" and an honor due to the Lawgiver.[23]

Forgiveness: Pardon vs. Payment

In his anthology of Edwardsean works on the atonement (including Jonathan Maxcy's), Edwards Amasa Park suggested that "the most distinguishing feature of the 'new divinity' is, that it gives a prominence to God as a Sovereign in applying and conducting, as well as originating the redemptive work."[24] The idea of divine sovereignty is the abiding principle which informs nearly every aspect of the moral governmental theory of the atonement. According

---

Crisp explains, "In this context, *rectoral justice* is that aspect of divine justice whereby God rightly governs the cosmos in accordance with his moral law. *Retributive justice* is that aspect of divine justice whereby God's wrath is meted out to those creatures who transgress the moral law, who remain the objects of divine wrath and are not the objects of divine mercy" (Crisp, "Penal Non-Substitution," 140–41).

22. Furman, "Alexander Hamilton," 233.
23. Furman, "Of Growth in Grace," 553.
24. "Introductory Essay," in Park, *Atonement*, xii.

to this scheme, forgiveness is designed to accentuate the maximum amount of sovereignty and freedom to God such that he is not obligated to save anyone nor can anyone demand anything from him. While most Edwardseans denied the transfer of righteousness or the literal payment of a debt in order to safeguard divine sovereignty, Furman still affirmed imputation in a way that many New Divinity men did not. As has been demonstrated, his doctrine of atonement was indeed a theological blend. Nevertheless, the sovereignty of God was certainly a central theme in his thinking. Furman spoke often about the "sovereign and free grace of God" and the "sovereign mercy" of the Moral Governor.[25] His sermons routinely included thoughts concerning the "honor of God's moral government" and "the honor of the true God infinitely good."[26] Furman painstakingly defended the glory, honor, and sovereignty of God around every turn. He even exhorted his listeners to "entertain exalted thoughts of God's moral government."[27]

This theme of sovereignty conformed well to his idea of pardon. God is an infallible judge and moral governor who owes absolutely nothing to the sinner. It is not God's duty to forgive. At the core of divine pardon is the freedom of God, and Furman protected this idea at all costs. He preached of the "pardoning mercy" of God and "the great sovereign of all worlds, beheld with mercy and complacency."[28] Moral government and pardon strongly appealed to Furman because they allowed divine grace to be a completely unilateral exercise, not dependent upon the sinner. Christ satisfied divine justice so that his forgiveness could be a free act, not a compelled one. God is, in some sense, bound by his justice. However, Furman sought to maintain sovereign grace which was consistent with divine justice. He asked, "Are we not the creatures of God, and indebted to him for every blessing and advantage we enjoy, as well as for our existence? And has he not a sovereign right to demand our services?"[29] This significant Creator-creature distinction undergirded Furman's understanding of pardon. Like the New Divinity, divine sovereignty is the overarching issue behind the glory of the atonement.

Furman's reticence to utilize the language of "payment" stems from this principle of sovereignty. If Christ's work can be monetized or commercialized in some way, grace is eviscerated because sinners can theoretically

25. Furman, "Constitution and Order," 262, 275.

26. Furman, "Of Infant Salvation," 593; Richard Furman, "Oration, Delivered at the Charleston Orphan-House," 360.

27. Furman, "Sermon, Occasioned by the Death of the Honorable Major General Alexander Hamilton," 238.

28. Furman, "Unity and Peace," 292; Furman, "Oration, Delivered at the Charleston Orphan-House," 362.

29. Furman, "Rewards of Grace," 330.

claim their salvation at judgment instead of pleading for it as humble subjects of God's moral government. This was the belief of the Edwardseans. Jonathan Edwards Jr., believed by some to be the founder of the American moral governmental theory of the atonement, evinced the New Divinity view when he wrote, "Christ did not, in the literal sense, pay the debt we owed to God; if he had paid it, all grace would have been excluded from the pardon of the sinner."[30] Due to Furman's hesitancy to use commercial language of payment and his eagerness to speak of "pardon," it is reasonable to assume he shared this same sentiment. In other words, at the very least, Furman believed that the idea of divine pardon emphasized sovereign grace much more than the idea of payment. The goal of the gospel in Furman's mind is a "humble dependence on divine grace."[31]

Theologians like Jonathan Edwards Jr. did not recognize an exchange of righteousness in the atonement. Like many other Edwardseans, he rejected distributive justice. According to Edwards the younger, none "will pretend that commutative justice is satisfied by Christ; for the controversy between God and the sinner is not concerning property. Nor is distributive justice satisfied. If it were, there would be no more grace in the discharge of the sinner, than there is in the discharge of a criminal, when he hath endured the full punishment to which, according to law, he hath been condemned."[32] In other words, Edwards Jr. believed that if Christ's righteousness can be personally imputed or distributed to sinners, then sinners have already been saved and judgment is a charade. However, as has been shown, Furman affirmed distributive justice and the personal imputation of Christ's righteousness. Therefore, his view of the atonement is not a strict New Divinity view. Furman was motivated by the sovereignty of God, however, he did not deny a transfer of merits like other Edwardseans. Furman preached of believers' "humble reliance on the Savior's merit and grace."[33] Thus, although Furman shied away from the language of payment, he did not create a great divide between the atonement and salvation itself. This created points of tension in his doctrine of atonement that will be discussed later.

Substitution vs. Non-Substitution

The work of Oliver Crisp concerning "non-penal substitution" and "penal non-substitution" sheds further light on Furman's unique governmental

---

30. Edwards, "Grace Consistent with Atonement," in Park, *Atonement*, 18.
31. Furman, "Conversion Essential to Salvation," 438.
32. Edwards, "Inferences and Reflections," in Park, *Atonement*, 37.
33. Furman, "Conversion Essential to Salvation," 426.

substitutionary view, demonstrating its resemblance to some views while also distancing it from others. According to Crisp, Hugo Grotius, the jurist and scholar who is attributed with developing the first moral governmental view, was himself not exclusively governmental. Crisp explains,

> The Dutch Arminian lawyer-theologian Hugo Grotius (1583–1645) is often credited with first articulating it, but his view is not as clearly "governmental" as some commentators seem to believe it to be. It may be that Grotius's doctrine of the atonement was more like a species of penal substitution with elements that sound like the developed governmental view of the atonement. ... In this case, Grotius's doctrine is a sort of theological hybrid, or at least an intermediate species of atonement theory.[34]

Therefore, Furman was not the first to integrate parts of moral governmental and penal substitutionary atonement. In some ways, he shared a similar view with Hugo Grotius. Both men adhered to a "hybrid" theory of the atonement that emphasized the vindication of God's moral government. However, Furman's doctrine of atonement had much more in common with that of the New Divinity, the first indigenous theological school in America.[35] Crisp distinguishes the Grotian governmental theory of the atonement from this "Edwardsian" governmental view, named after Jonathan Edwards Jr. in the nineteenth century.[36] The American understanding of the governmental theory, which Crisp calls "penal non-substitution," was substantially different than the Grotian view. Crisp compares the two theories of governmental atonement and finds their similarities and differences:

> So, unlike the Grotian view, the Edwardsian view states that the punishment of sin is an obligation, at least in the sense that once God has created the sort of world he has, it is incumbent upon God to ensure that either sin is punished in the person of the sinner, or some suitable act of atonement is made in the person of a vicar. Where the Edwardsian and Grotian views agree, it is concerning the notion that rectoral justice *must* be satisfied whereas retributive justice *may* be relaxed, so that Christ's atonement satisfies the former, not the latter, such that this constitutes an act rectorally sufficient for the vindication of divine justice and the upholding of divine moral government, consistent with the moral law. This is a very important

---

34. Crisp, "Penal Non-Substitution," 140–41.
35. Conforti, *Samuel Hopkins and the New Divinity Movement*, vii.
36. Crisp, "Penal Non-Substitution," 141.

component of penal non-substitution. It means that rectoral justice is somehow more fundamental to the nature of God than retributive justice is.[37]

Furman's insistence upon punishment for sin indicates a particularly "penal" nature to his doctrine of atonement consistent with both historical views of moral governmental theory. Furman also emphasized the necessity of rectoral justice in a way that Grotius and Edwards did. However, against the Grotian and Edwardsian views of governmental atonement, it appears that the Furmanian atonement is also unique in some ways. While penal and governmental in nature, Richard Furman's doctrine of atonement does not necessarily qualify as "penal non-substitution." His doctrine of atonement is neither Grotian nor Edwardsean. It can be more properly described as "governmental substitution."

Like Hugo Grotius, Furman clearly integrated elements of penal atonement and moral governmental atonement. However, unlike Grotius, Furman's doctrine of atonement does not sacrifice the integrity of the penal substitutionary theory. Thus his "hybrid" theory was not of the same species.[38] Like Edwardseans such as Jonathan Edwards Jr., Furman put a heavy emphasis upon the obligatory nature of the law and the necessity of the atonement in a way that Grotius did not. For instance, Furman spoke of the "penal demands" of the law and the "unspeakable obligations that man is under to him."[39] He insisted that faith "believes that God is holy, just, and true; that his wrath is provoked by the sins of men."[40] According to Furman, to believe that God is just is to believe that God metes out his wrath upon sin.

Although Richard Furman preferred the covenantal language of "representative" and "head" to that of "substitute," the idea of substitution is latent throughout his soteriology, primarily in the paschal imagery of the Bible. For instance, Furman referred to the church as the "Lambs of that

37. Crisp, "Penal Non-Substitution," 149.

38. Furman's merging of moral governmental and penal substitutionary theory are indeed reminiscent of Jonathan Edwards. Oliver Crisp explains, "The evidence suggests that the seeds of the New England governmental view of the atonement were sown by Edwards himself. But he did not have the opportunity, or perhaps the inclination, to develop this in his own work. So the views expressed by Bellamy, Samuel Hopkins, and Jonathan Edwards, Jr., to name the three most important exponents of the doctrine among the theologians of the New Divinity, were, one might think, a doctrine innovation in one respect. But they were building on some ideas latent in the work of Edwards Senior, and they did, it appears, have his sanction for doing so" (Crisp, "Moral Government of God," 78–79.)

39. Furman, "On Growth in Grace," 553; Furman, "Unity and Peace," 312.

40. Furman, "Royal Marriage Feast," 470.

Flock for which the Savior laid down his life."[41] In describing the "moderate" Calvinism of his dear friend Edmund Botsford, Furman recounted, "To the awakened, and penitent, he affectionately pointed out the Lamb of God, which taketh away the sin of the world; and published free grace and salvation in his name."[42] This was the doctrine of substitution in Richard Furman's Calvinism, not explicit but implicit. In his work *Defending Substitution: An Essay on Atonement in Paul* (2015), Simon Gathercole defines substitutionary atonement as "Christ's death in our place, instead of us."[43] Furman affirmed this definition of substitution, even when the word substitution was not necessarily present in his writings. His version of moral governmental theory, while lacking commercial imagery, emphasized the fact that Christ died as a lamb in the place of sinners.

What remains is to demonstrate exactly how Furman defined the nature of Christ's substitution. For instance, in Leviticus 16, while the scapegoat could be considered a sacrificial substitution, it does not endure a penalty of any kind. In other words, it serves a non-penal substitution upon which the sins of the people are carried off. While Furman clearly supported the ideas of punishment, headship, representation, "transaction," and even a broadly limited atonement view, his lack of explicit substitution language leaves lingering questions as to how he integrated moral government and penal substitution.

Although clearly distancing himself from traditional moral governmental views with doctrines such as imputation, how did Furman account for the substitutionary character of the atonement? Did Christ's death in the place of the elect merely make amends for sin or did he actually absorb the consequences of sin? Moreover, was his substitution also one of penance as in other moral governmental views? Answering such questions is key to understanding if Furman was able to sustain both moral governmental and penal substitutionary models in their integrity instead of simply borrowing elements from both in order to produce a Grotian blend.

The substitutionary quality of Richard Furman's doctrine of atonement becomes evident when juxtaposed with McLeod Campbell's doctrine of vicarious penitence, another substitutionary model of the atonement. In this view, Christ atones for sin by repenting on behalf of fallen sinners. Therefore, Oliver Crisp has appropriately labeled this theory of atonement "non-penal substitution" because, as Crisp rightly observes, "vicarious

---

41. Furman, "Of Infant Salvation," 601.
42. Furman, "Rev. Edmund Botsford," 462.
43. Gathercole, *Defending Substitution*, 15.

penitence is only one aspect of this doctrine of the atonement."[44] According to many, this view countervails the weaknesses of penal substitution by maintaining the substitutionary quality of the atonement without the penalty of sin. Crisp explains,

> The central insight of defenders of this sort of view is that it offers a doctrine of the atonement that preserves the substitutionary character of penal substitution beloved of the Reformed tradition, whilst avoiding some of the problems associated with the penal aspect of the penal substitutionary view. To put it bluntly, penal substitution is often criticized for requiring that divine justice be met by a substitute able to take upon himself the penal consequences for the sin of human beings (or some number of human beings less than the totality of humanity.) Some think this paints God as an uncaring and bloodthirsty tyrant; one who demands that justice is satisfied when it was within his gift to exercise grace and mercy instead. Others think that this view of the atonement does not adequately reflect the complex of biblical images used to explain the atonement. Still others question the coherence of claiming that one person can take upon himself the penal consequences of the sin of another. What defenders of non-penal substitution maintain is that Christ's work might involve a substitutionary element—particularly, though not exclusively, vicarious penitence—without assumption of the penal consequences of human sin that is so repugnant to some, and so baffling to others.[45]

Crisp insightfully recognizes that the event of a substitution in the atonement does not necessarily involve a vicar taking upon himself the penal consequences of sin. Theoretically, one could stand in the place of sinners and repent on their behalf. In the case of McLeod Campbell, the divine substitute is not a slaughtered lamb that physically endures the holy anger of God against sin; he is a penitent lamb who experiences "in reference to their sin, and present to God on their behalf, an adequate sorrow and repentance."[46] In other words, in the doctrine of non-penal substitution, Jesus is a non-penalized substitute. He is, rather, a pleading substitute.

As Crisp points out, this view is not without its own weaknesses. For instance, if a morally blameless person cannot take upon himself the penal consequences of someone else's sin, how is a vicarious apology more feasible or valid? Could such penitence be of infinite worth before an offended God?

---

44. Crisp, "Non-Penal Substitution," 417.
45. Crisp, "Non-Penal Substitution," 417–18.
46. Crisp, "Non-Penal Substitution," 416.

Campbell's idea of vicarious penitence leaves much to explain. However, despite its soteriological lacunae, the doctrine of non-penal substitution does serve to cast light on the concept of reparation. Can a sinless Christ make reparation for sin by substituting himself for sinners but *not* receive punishment in the place of fallen human beings? Can there be meaningful substitution without penalty? According to Richard Furman's strict understanding of retributive justice, divine justice does not permit forgiveness without satisfaction, and satisfaction necessarily entails "penal demands." In Furman's words, there is a punishment that is "due to sin."[47] Therefore, godly sorrow, even by a morally blameless person, cannot satisfy divine justice if it does not include punishment of some kind. Contrary to Campbell, Furman did not believe that an apology or repentance met the "claims of justice." There must be proportionality between the crime committed and the punishment allotted. For Furman, the atonement did more than simply make reparations for sin; Christ satisfied the "demand" of justice by taking upon himself the punishment for sin. Richard Furman integrated penal, substitutionary, and moral governmental elements into his doctrine of the atonement by emphasizing these dual elements of rectoral and retributive justice; however, one other concept was equally critical for Furman: propitiation.

As Simon Gathercole has rightly observed, the concept of substitution "is logically distinguishable from related concepts such as penalty, representation, expiation, and propitiation."[48] However, like most Calvinistic Baptists, Richard Furman affirmed propitiation as essential to penal substitutionary atonement. While propitiation and substitution are "logically distinguishable" concepts, Furman's doctrine of propitiation heavily implied substitution. In Furman's doctrine of atonement, propitiation was necessarily substitutionary. But in Furman's governmental substitutionary model, propitiation was not simply about meting out wrath; it was also about upholding moral government. In the Furmanian atonement, propitiation becomes a simultaneous act of rectoral and retributive justice. In his sermon entitled "On the Analogy Between the Dispensations of Grace by the Gospel, and a Royal Marriage Feast," Furman lamented that the unbelieving soul has "no atonement that it can make to propitiate the Divine Majesty, and procure deliverance from the dreadful curse of his violated law."[49] In this instance, Furman's use of "Divine Majesty" is similar to his use of divine honor. As will be shown, the Charleston pastor considered "majesty" and "honor" as virtual synonyms. Furman interpreted propitiation as not simply

---

47. Furman, "Of Growth in Grace," 553.
48. Gathercole, *Defending Substitution*, 18.
49. Furman, "Royal Marriage Feast," 470.

an averting of God's wrath by a divine substitute; it was also an appeasing and honoring of a Moral Lawgiver.

In the above passage, Furman's use of "Divine Majesty" as the direct object of the verb "propitiate" clearly indicates that he understood Christ to be suffering in some way for sinners in their stead. His atonement is propitiatory and thus substitutionary in nature. Furman believed Christ to be averting the wrath and satisfying the justice of the "Divine Majesty" by taking upon himself the penal consequences of sin. Therefore, unlike McLeod Campbell's doctrine of vicarious penitence, Furman's concept of substitution does not merely imply expiation of, or making amends for, sin. The Furmanian atonement is not simply doing penance for the wrong committed; it is propitiatory. For Furman, propitiation was inextricable from the idea of an offended Lawgiver. Thus, he concluded that Christ's propitiatory atonement "procure(d) deliverance from the dreadful curse of [God's] violated law." In his sermon "Conversion Essential to Salvation," Furman similarly linked propitiation with justification when he preached that forgiveness of sins "is expressive of justification, and peace with God, through Christ's obedience, and propitiatory sacrifice: the benefits of which are applied to the souls of real penitents and believers."[50] This moral governmental understanding of propitiation is another reason that Furman preferred to describe the atonement in terms of pardon rather than in commercial terms of payment.

Furman integrated rectoral and retributive justice in his doctrine of atonement in such a way that he acknowledged a public vindication of the law while also affirming a private reparation for sin itself in Christ's "propitiatory sacrifice." Juxtaposed with Crisp's "non-penal substitution" and "penal non-substitution" models, it becomes clear that Furman believed that moral governmental and penal substitutionary theories of the atonement were not only compatible, they implied each other. Therefore, his view should be described as "governmental substitution" for its balancing of both theories. Daniel W. Cooley and Douglas A. Sweeney have recently critiqued Oliver Crisp's assertion that the American moral governmental theory is a "penal non-substitution."[51] Instead, they have soundly labeled the Edwardsean view of the atonement a "*non-distributive* form of penal substitution," insisting that the New Divinity school understood Christ's substitution as one made for punishments, not people.[52] In this sense, Furman distanced

50. Furman, "Conversion Essential to Salvation," 433.

51. Crisp, "Penal Non-Substitution," 140–68.

52. Cooley and Sweeney explain, "Instead of Christ being the substitute victim for man, Christ's sufferings are substituted for man's punishment. Instead of the atonement being distributed to each one of God's elect individually, it is construed as a collective satisfaction for all who believe" (Cooley and Sweeney, "Edwardseans and the

himself from the New Divinity, affirming a distributive form of penal substitution, but not emphasizing substitution in the way that others did.

The Application of the Atonement: Furman, Johnson, and Boyce

In order to gather a better sense of Furman's specific theory of the atonement, Furman will be juxtaposed with two Calvinistic Southern Baptists, one who did uphold an exclusively moral governmental view and one who did not. The atonement theories of James Petigru Boyce (1827–1888) and William Bullein Johnson (1782–1862) provide an opportunity to throw Furman's doctrine of atonement into theological relief for the sake of better understanding the finer points of his thinking.

James P. Boyce eschewed any kind of moral governmental view as it was traditionally understood in the eighteenth and nineteenth centuries. In his *Abstract*, Boyce defends what he simply calls the "Calvinistic theory" of the atonement. According to Boyce, this theory "is that of Calvin and the churches which he established. It is the theory of the Regular Baptists of the past. No other prevailed among those who have held distinctively Calvinistic Baptist sentiments until the days of Andrew Fuller. He, because of his great ability, contributed greatly to the acceptance of the modification which we have just been considering."[53] Boyce was not averse to calling Christ's atonement an "official substitution."[54] Like Furman, he affirmed Christ as the "legal representative of his people and their covenant head" wherein He "has made a real atonement for us."[55] However, unlike Furman, Boyce used heavy pecuniary language in his descriptions of the atonement. Christ's deity "gave infinite value to suffering."[56] On another occasion, Boyce affirmed that Christ, "as so substituted, paid the penalty" for the elect.[57] These concepts enabled Boyce to apply a more precise extent of the atonement than Furman's moderate Calvinism would allow.

While Boyce's doctrine of atonement as a whole is beyond the aim of this monograph, his critique of governmental theory provides an opportunity to engage Boyce and Furman in theological conversation for the

---

Atonement," 122.

53. Boyce, *Abstract of Systematic Theology*, 317.
54. Boyce, *Abstract of Systematic Theology*, 324.
55. Boyce, *Abstract of Systematic Theology*, 325, 319.
56. Boyce, *Abstract of Systematic Theology*, 328.
57. Boyce, *Abstract of Systematic Theology*, 333.

purpose of elucidating Furman's exact positions on sin and the atonement. According to Boyce,

> Those who hold this theory maintain that God cannot consistently forgive sin upon mere repentance and faith; but that the necessity for its punishment does not arise from the nature of God, and his abhorrence of sin; wherefore there is no principle in him which requires all sin to be punished for itself alone; but from the necessity which exists for maintaining his moral government in the universe.[58]

Boyce's first two critiques echoed this point. In his first objection, Boyce inveighed against "the nature" which the governmental theory "ascribes to sin." He continues, "It does not regard it essential that all sin should be punished. Therefore sin does not in itself intrinsically deserve punishment." Boyce's second point seems to finish his thought: "It places the punishment of sin on a wrong basis, namely, the good of the universe as involved in the moral government of God; and not because it deserves punishment as sin."[59]

Boyce seemed to suggest that one cannot punish sin both for the good of the moral universe *and* for the intrinsic evil within sin itself. However, Furman did not treat the two as if they were mutually exclusive ideas of sin. His reasoning was grounded in the distinction between the nature of sin and the effects of sin.

In describing the "evil of covetousness," Furman divided his discussion into two parts: "First, in its nature:—It is sin, a spiritual evil—a transgression of God's righteous law, the justice and equity of which it affronts; and it is directly opposed to the spirit and design of the gospel of Christ." Furman then explained, "It is a most deceitful evil, imposing on men under the names of prudence, frugality, and even justice; and deluding them with the hope and confidence of being happy in those enjoyments which are in their nature unsatisfying, and of but momentary duration."[60] Therefore, according to Furman, sin is not simply an evil; it is a "spiritual evil" that extends its vile grip well beyond what sinful humans can see or even realize. Due to its "deceitful evil," sin both affronts the law of God and opposes the gospel of Christ.

However, according to Furman, the nature of sin is only half of its evil. Furman continued,

---

58. Boyce, *Abstract of Systematic Theology*, 309.
59. Boyce, *Abstract of Systematic Theology*, 309.
60. Furman, "On Covetousness," 576.

> Secondly. In its effects—With respect to God; our fellow creatures; and ourselves. It affronts the majesty of God, by rebelling against his authority, by rejecting the counsels of his wisdom, by disregarding the rule of his justice, and by undervaluing what he has appointed to be the supreme object of our affection, and true source of our happiness—even himself.[61]

In addition to its inherent evil, sin is so wicked that it goes public with its wickedness, infecting others and their respective views of God. Sin is a private and public affair, direct and indirect. Therefore, for Furman, the issue was not that sin isn't "intrinsically" evil, to borrow Boyce's language. The problem is that sin is also *extrinsically* evil. It is never self-contained. For this reason, it requires a public as well as a private response from the offended Moral Lawgiver. The Furmanian atonement deals simultaneously with the "nature" of sin as well as with the "effects" of sin, punishing sin for its own sake while also vindicating the "disregarded" character of God's moral government.

Boyce's third critique touched on the governmental view of the nature of God himself: "God is here beheld, not as a righteous judge taking vengeance on the violators of his law, nor as a rightful king punishing those who have rejected his authority, but simply as a benevolent being entirely regardless of his own nature, or of the difference between right and wrong, punishing some men for the good of others."[62] In this objection, it seems that Boyce is determined to rightfully avoid sacrificing the justice of God for the benevolence of God. However, in this particular instance, he neglects the idea that God's benevolence is in fact part of "his own nature" and not necessarily contrary to his justice. Richard Furman certainly did not see the two at odds.

Furman was not opposed to referring to God as a "Righteous Judge."[63] In his eulogy of Alexander Hamilton, Furman spoke on the subject of death, and he could not avoid the subject of God's moral government: "Death was threatened as the punishment of sin, when the Great Creator, and Moral Governor, gave his first law to man: And its introduction, continuance, and power, afford convincing proof of the rebellion, guilt, and general depravity of the human race."[64] Furman continued, giving another reason for the entrance of death into a fallen world:

---

61. Furman, "On Covetousness," 576–77.
62. Boyce, *Abstract of Systematic Theology*, 309.
63. Furman, "Rewards of Grace," 332.
64. Furman, "Death's Dominion Over Man Considered," 232–33.

> Another reason, for our universal mortality, which may be inferred from the economy of God's moral government, is the restraint it lays on the passions and vices of men, by producing a salutary fear; which is of important use, not only in a moral and religious view, but in its influence on social and civil life; affording one of the most powerful sanctions to laws and government.[65]

As shown, Richard Furman did not treat the interests of God's moral government and the claims of divine justice as if they were diametrically opposed, as Boyce seems to insinuate in his *Abstract*. God's creation was good, and thus this arrangement was also good. In Furman's view, the Creator and Moral Governor of the universe first gave his law to man as an act of kindness to humanity. The moral law simultaneously displays the justice and benevolence of God. Therefore, Boyce's contention that the governmental model espouses a God who is a "benevolent being" who acts "entirely regardless of his own nature" was an unfair treatment, at least as it pertained to the Furmanian atonement. According to Furman's governmental substitutionary theory, God metes out his wrathful punishment upon sin in the crucified Christ because He is just and good and wise in his nature. His power is not an arbitrary power; it is consistent with his "natural and moral government."

In Boyce's fourth critique of the governmental view, he hypothetically contended, "Had God created one man, or one angel only, and had that angel sinned, there could have been no reason, either in the broken law, or in the dishonor to God, for his punishment, unless other beings were also to be created."[66] Boyce correctly identified the public nature of the moral governmental theory of the atonement. However, Boyce mistakenly assumed that the corporate element of the moral governmental view necessarily precluded God's personal displeasure with sin. Furman did not view these two aspects of the atonement as conflicting in any way. Once again, as shown in the earlier passage, the public-private theme emerged in Furman's thought, this time in his view of the law. The law is good for its immediate "punishment of sin" as well as for the "restraint it lays on the passions and vices of men, by producing a salutary fear." It is good for the sake of justice and it is even good for civilization itself.

The nature of sin and the effects of sin are both held in check in Richard Furman's moral governmental view of the atonement. In the law, God deals with sin for its own sake and provides containment of further sin. It is

---

65. Furman, "Death's Dominion," 233–34.
66. Boyce, *Abstract of Systematic Theology*, 309–10.

personal in its punishment and public in its corporate and civil good. Even Furman's unique phrase "salutary fear" suggests that goodness and justice were not contradictory categories when it comes to the divine law. As God himself is both just and good, so is his government. The atonement thus honors God as a righteous judge *and* as a benevolent king, not one or the other as Boyce seemed to suppose. God's moral government is more than about benevolence but about aloof his moral attributes.

While Furman's governmental substitution stood the test of Boyce's critiques, how does his version compare with William B. Johnson's more conventional moral governmental theory of the atonement? Juxtaposed with the likes of Johnson, does Furman appear to dilute some aspects of the governmental view? In 1822, Johnson preached a sermon before the Charleston Baptist Association entitled "Love Characteristic of the Deity" in which he unequivocally advocated a moral governmental view of the atonement. In this sermon, according to Michael Haykin, "Johnson spoke of the death of Christ in unmistakable New Divinity terms."[67]

Conspicuously absent from Johnson's sermon is the idea of imputation. Unlike Furman and more like Jonathan Maxcy, Johnson rejected the idea as unbiblical, at least in the soteriological sense.[68] This became the greatest theological canyon separating Furman's and Johnson's versions of moral governmental theory. Furman not only taught imputation in his sermons, affirmed it confessionally, and catechized the children of FBC Charleston in the doctrine; he also utilized biblical imagery in order to better inculcate the concept. For Johnson, salvation was not primarily about being accounted personally righteous by the active and passive obedience of Christ, but about God the Moral Governor vindicating his character in Christ, God's penal example, and lawfully establishing the means by which anyone could believe in Christ and no longer face condemnation. Johnson posited that the "idea" of the gospel is "the love of God as exercised towards man antecedent to the gift of his Son, and adopting a medium through which it might be manifested consistently with justice, his injured law, and the dignity of his throne."[69]

The concept of medium constitutes another significant departure Furman made from traditional nineteenth century moral governmental theory. In Furman's view, the atonement is not God's "medium" for salvation; it *is* salvation. Whereas Johnson referred to the atonement as "a full and adequate atonement to the violated law," Furman referred to it as a "complete

---

67. Haykin, "Great Admirers of the Transatlantic Divinity," 204.
68. Wills, *First Baptist Church of Columbia, South Carolina 1809 to 2002*, 48.
69. Johnson, "Love Characteristic of the Deity," 58.

atonement" whereby all conditions for salvation had been met.[70] Although subtle, the distinction could be further explained in another way. Whereas Johnson insisted that in the atonement "ample provision was made for the pardon of sin," Furman instead contended that a personal salvation had actually been accomplished, requiring personal "application" to be effected.[71] The atonement is more than a provision for pardon; it *is* pardon.

According to Furman, all of Christ's blessings "are secured to them by the same covenant, together with pardon by his blood, justification by his righteousness, and access to God through his intercession."[72] Pardon is "secured" at the atonement, not merely offered. Similar to Andrew Fuller, who also upheld a penal substitutionary view, Furman is able to balance his Calvinism inside of a governmental system by emphasizing the idea of application.

The concepts of imputation and application that distinguished the Furmanian atonement from that of Johnson were also supplemented by yet another chief theme in Furman's soteriology: union. Johnson's moral governmental view lacked a robust doctrine of union, at least in the way that Furman employed it. For Johnson, Christ is not so much an organic "head" united to his people as he is the Redeemer to "maintain the dignity and preserve the rights of God's moral government."[73] Conversely, the idea of union allowed Furman to integrate penal substitutionary motifs into his doctrine of atonement without explicitly mentioning imputation. Because Christ is united to his people in the covenant of grace, the benefits of the atonement will be ineluctably applied to the elect. Furman upheld the view that the "Divine Spirit" effects this "union with Christ."[74] Johnson held to the New Divinity view that human sin is located chiefly in the sinner's sinning, not necessarily in being accounted sinful. However, Furman considered all of humanity a "mass of fallen nature" whereby God "entailed on them the guilt and depravity of Adam."[75] For Furman, with the help of the doctrine of union, imputation extended both ways: from Adam to the world, and from Jesus to the elect, "united, in one grand assembly, to their glorious Head."[76]

---

70. Johnson, "Love Characteristic of the Deity," 58; Furman, "America's Deliverance and Duty," 403.
71. Johnson, "Love Characteristic of the Deity," 65.
72. Furman, "On Growth in Grace," 554.
73. Johnson, "Love Characteristic of the Deity," 52.
74. Furman, "Unity and Peace," 290.
75. Furman, "Of Infant Salvation," 594.
76. Furman, "Constitution and Order," 284.

However, despite this and other differences, Johnson's doctrine of the atonement approaches that of Furman in several ways, most notably in their common emphasis upon the atonement as a pardon instead of a payment. Johnson shared Furman's aversion to commercial tropes in describing the atonement. But Johnson's was much more than an aversion to pecuniary concepts; it was an outright rejection: "Considered in the point of view, just exhibited, full atonement is perfectly consistent with free pardon; for it is not the payment of the sinner's debt on the principles of pecuniary or commercial justice, but a satisfaction to moral justice, to open the way for the consistent exercise of mercy."[77] Whereas Furman generally distanced himself from commercial concepts, Johnson eschewed them entirely.

Another aspect of Johnson's theology that mirrored Furman's is the publicity of both sin and the atonement itself, another distinguishing feature of the moral governmental model. In praising the "the great moral Governor of the Universe, in whom all his creatures live, move, and have their being," Johnson described the divine administration in this way:

> Under his government, then, an equal and just administration will be obtained; and the virtuous and good will have nothing to fear. But prostrate the dignity of its holy Governor, abase his glory, and you destroy the rights, the liberties, and the happiness of its subjects. You introduce misery, wretchedness, and eternal ruin. You open the way for the annihilation of the Universe.[78]

For Johnson, like Furman, an offense against the Moral Governor is likewise a moral dissolution of society. It dishonors God and destroys civilization. Sin introduces more sin. In other words, it is both personal and public. Johnson believed that sin wasn't simply a moral destruction; it was also ontological, paving the way "for the annihilation of the Universe." Furman seemed to share this view when he spoke of Christ as the "offended and injured God" who would appear "in that tremendous day, 'when the heavens shall pass away with a great noise;' the earth be thrown into convulsions and wrapped in flames, the sun extinguished, and the stars dissolved."[79] In some sense, Furman viewed heaven itself as a restoration of God's honor and the preservation of a godly society in which the publicly sinister effects of sin are undone. The public and private theme is pervasive in both Furman and Johnson's writings, indicating another distinguishing feature of the moral governmental theory of the atonement.

77. Johnson, "Love Characteristic of the Deity," 60.
78. Johnson, "Love Characteristic of the Deity," 48.
79. Furman, "Constitution and Order," 285.

This personal-public dynamic lead to a third distinguishing feature of moral governmental theory that both Furman and Johnson undoubtedly shared: the glory of the Moral Governor and the good of his subjects as inextricably linked. In other words, neither Furman nor Johnson viewed divine doxology and human pleasure as mutually exclusive. Johnson explained, "Now in making his glory the chief object of his pursuit, Jehovah affords a clear proof of his nature as a God of love, or infinite benevolence. For ultimately and inseparably connected with the accomplishment of this object, is the preservation of his government, and the happiness of his creatures."[80] Due to the public nature of sin, the atonement is both an open vindication of the good character of the Moral Governor as well as a restoration of the plight of the denizens under his governmental authority. Furman affirmed the same principle when he averred, "The end of the gospel ministry, is, in subordination to the glory of the God, the edification and perfecting of the saints."[81] Furman's view of ministry was not a proto-prosperity gospel. It defined pleasure not in terms of worldly self-gratification but in terms of the character of God's moral government. In this scheme, even God's displeasure with sin is an expression of his good character.

Ultimately, Furman and Johnson affirmed many of the same principles in their respective moral governmental theories of the atonement. Each Baptist theologian preferred judicial over commercial tropes, both emphasized the publicity of sin and the atonement, and they mutually insisted that the good of the saints is not at theological odds with the glory of the Moral Governor. Both South Carolinians greatly emphasized the moral government of God in a way that accentuated the rectoral justice of God. For instance, in his infamous treatise entitled *Exposition of the Views of the Baptists Relative to the Colored Population of the United States in A Communication to the Governor of South Carolina*, Furman tragically defended the practice of slavery to the South Carolina governor by appealing to the Moral Governor of the Universe: "For a sense of the Divine Government has a meliorating influence on the minds of men, restraining them from crime, and disposing them to virtuous action. To those also, who are humbled before the Heavenly Majesty for their sins, and learn to be thankful for his mercies, the Divine Favor is manifested. From them judgments are averted, and on them blessings are bestowed."[82] Like Johnson (who also defended the practice of slavery), Furman understood Christ's death in terms of governmental

---

80. Johnson, "Love Characteristic of the Deity," 47.

81. Furman, "Constitution and Order," 277.

82. Furman, *Exposition of the Views of the Baptists, Relative to the Colored Population of the United States*, 4.

pardon or "divine favor" by which one avoided the condemnation of the law and received mercy from the Divine Majesty.

However, despite their agreement on moral government and divine pardon, Johnson's view of rectoral justice proved much different than Furman's, namely concerning the atonement itself. Since Johnson viewed the atonement as a "means" and not necessarily as a real atonement by which salvation was secured, he detached the love of God from the atonement in a way that Furman did not. In a somewhat provocative statement, Johnson insisted,

> In itself considered, the atonement of Christ does not deliver any soul from condemnation. It is the interest which the soul has in the benefits of the atonement that effects this deliverance; an interest that depends not upon the principle of atonement, but upon that by which it has been provided, and in which it originates, viz.: Love, or infinite benevolence, under the influence of which, this interest will be imparted according to the righteous and sovereign will of God. For he will have mercy, on whom he will have mercy, and he will have compassion on whom he will have compassion.[83]

Richard Furman could not have uttered such a statement. While Furman clearly affirmed the "sovereign will of God" in pardoning sinners and God's love in doing so, he never detached the atonement from the actual reconciliation of sinners with God and God with sinners. As a confessional Calvinist, Furman viewed the "principle of atonement" as the real reconciliation of individual sinners. According to Furman, "Reconciliation to God, through the mediation of his son, comprehends, the pardon of our sins, the justification of our persons, renovation of our nature, adoption into the heavenly family, and a title to eternal life."[84] All of these are effected through Christ's mediatorial death. Therefore, the cross is the centerpiece of the Furmanian atonement. By looking to the atonement, Furman believed that sinners behold the love of God and need not look past it. The essence of faith, according to Furman, "consists in a firm persuasion, on the testimony of heaven, that Jesus is the Son of God, and the only Savior of men; and in such a reliance on his justifying righteousness, atoning blood, and living intercession, as causes us to cleave to him as the anchor of our hope, the ark of our safety, and city of our refuge." [85] At no time does Furman insist that true saving faith must include something beyond a "trust" in the atoning work

---

83. Johnson, "Love Characteristic of the Deity," 60.
84. Furman, "Death's Dominion Over Man Considered," 237.
85. Furman, "Death's Dominion Over Man Considered," 236.

of Christ. While the unconditional love of God is assumed by Furman to be the most eternal, unalterable, efficient cause of salvation, it is not listed as an essential object of faith as if it could somehow be wrested from the atonement itself.

Underneath these seemingly subtle differences in moral governmental theories of the atonement lies Johnson's rejection of the doctrine of imputation and its corollary view of rectoral justice. Despite the fact that Furman clearly accentuated rectoral justice in the law and moral government of God, he was not above referring to the eschatological judgment as "the great day of final retribution," when sinners will individually receive the penal consequences of their sin.[86] For Furman, God was much more than a Governor; he was also the just Judge of all the earth. This is one aspect of the "fixed" Calvinism that Furman shared with Oliver Hart and not with William B. Johnson. Consequently, the term "governmental substitution" appears to be the most suitable name one could apply to Furman's doctrine of atonement, for its blend of moral governmental and penal substitutionary models.

---

86. Furman, "Rewards of Grace," 341.

5

Critical Analysis of Furman's Doctrine of Atonement

Strengths and Weaknesses

SIX DAYS AFTER HIS death, Richard Furman's Charleston congregation published a tribute to their beloved preacher. In their tribute, the members of First Baptist Church praised Furman's tenderness as a pastor and the tenor of his theology: "He seldom or never engaged in religious controversy; though he always maintained the doctrines of the church with firmness and energy, yet with courtesy and affability; and if he failed to convince, he never offended . . . Such was our deceased pastor. But he has fulfilled his day; we are bereaved; and a thousand aching hearts are at this moment testifying their sorrow and his worth."[1] Richard Furman's ecumenical, non-controversial spirit imbued both his ministry and his theology. He was a conciliatory Calvinist. It was also evident at his funeral. Furman had ministers of other denominations preach at the service. He was a peacemaker, not a sectarian. As a result, one of the greatest strengths of Furman's doctrine of atonement was his ability to recognize the multi-dimensional nature of Christ's atoning work. He addressed the atonement in covenantal terms, governmental terms, legal terms, royal terms, and sacerdotal terms, just to name a few.[2] He believed all of these themes to be found in the Bible, his preeminent source for knowledge of divine things. Furman was skeptical of "systems,"

---

1. *Charleston Mercury and Morning Advertiser*, September 1, 1825, cited in Rogers, *Richard Furman*, 258.

2. Furman, "Children of Church Members," 489; Furman, "Royal Marriage Feast," 467–69; Furman, "An Oration," 362; Furman, "On Growth in Grace," 553.

excepting the great cosmic system of the Moral Governor. Although some traditional Calvinists may have overlooked the lawful nature of Christ's work and the honor paid to the Moral Governor of the universe, Furman did not. Although some moderate Calvinists insisted that Christ's death was merely a "medium" to salvation, Furman contended that the atonement was an actual saving act applied by faith. In many ways, Richard Furman attempted to bring together the strengths of both moral governmental and penal substitutionary theories into one blended view of the atonement.

Due to his non-controversial spirit, Furman chose to emphasize those aspects of Christ's work which accorded best with "the freeness of the Gospel call" rather than stir up contentious theological debate.[3] Although he was a Calvinist in the mold of *The Charleston Confession*, Furman preferred the language of "complete atonement" and "the all-sufficiency of the Savior's merit" instead of "limited atonement."[4] His doctrine of atonement was consistent with *The Charleston Confession*, but not in a rigid way. Furman's relentless commitment to the "honor of God's moral government" was proof of his willingness to inject the modern ideas of his age into a confessional framework.[5] In other words, Furman was a confessional Calvinist, but he was not necessarily bound by confessional language or concepts. Like other moral governmental Calvinists of his generation, Furman co-opted the "moral discourse of the Enlightenment," pouring modern wine into old Calvinist wineskins for the sake of advancing the gospel.[6]

Richard Furman was also a theological bridge-builder. From his friendship with Jonathan Maxcy to his tutelage of William B. Johnson to his correspondence with James Manning to his admiration for Andrew Fuller, Furman was a confessional Calvinist with an affection for New Divinity men who did not necessarily share all of his views. While Furman was not an adherent of the New Divinity, he sympathized greatly with their theology. Consequently, Furman's doctrine of atonement was an eclectic blend of confessional and Edwardsean theology, the likes of which had never been seen before in American Baptist life. On the one hand, Furman held firmly to the traditional Calvinist notion of imputed righteousness and the federal headship of Adam.[7] On the other hand, he believed that the goal of the atonement was to "corroborate the design of [God's] gospel, and promote

---

3. Furman, "Royal Marriage Feast," 466.
4. Furman, "On Growth in Grace," 553.
5. Furman, "Of Infant Salvation," 593.
6. Valeri, *Law and Providence in Joseph Bellamy's New England*, 42.
7. Furman, "On Growth in Grace," 553; Furman, "Of Infant Salvation," 592–94.

CRITICAL ANALYSIS OF FURMAN'S DOCTRINE OF ATONEMENT 91

the interest of his moral government."[8] To sin, Furman wrote, is "to charge the Great Moral Governor with having delivered a defective system."[9] Therefore, in Furman's view, the atonement was both an act of real justice under the law and a vindication of the Lawgiver himself. These were not mutually exclusive ideas in his mind.

Another of Richard Furman's strengths was his ability to retool the language of the confessions for his own moral governmental purposes. While the phrase "moral government" is absent from *The Charleston Confession*, a host of other words in *The Confession* were conducive to his moral governmental scheme.[10] In this way, Furman was not an original thinker so much as he was a theological renovator, giving fresh meaning to old confessional terms. For instance, the word "pardon" is used several times in *The Confession* to describe the forgiveness of sin in Christ.[11] The word "honor" is also employed to describe the nature of obedience to the Creator.[12] The nature of God's moral law and its reflection of God's authority is outlined as well.[13] All of these words supported Furman's quest to steer the work of Christ toward the glory of the Moral Governor. As a result, he clearly favored these ideas over others.

However, despite Furman's adherence to the Baptist confessions, he downplayed certain confessional themes because they did not conform to his moral governmental matrix. This was certainly one of his theological weaknesses. Although Furman exhibited a synthesis of different themes and tropes in his doctrine of atonement, others were noticeably lacking. Due to his governmental commitments, Richard Furman was not equitable in his use of confessional theology. For instance, in *The Charleston Confession*, pecuniary and commercial images are used quite frequently to describe the work of Christ. Words like "purchase," "price," "paid," and "surety" are laden throughout *The Confession*.[14] However, Furman routinely chose not to describe the atonement in these terms. His was an un-commercialized atonement, devoid of almost any monetary language whatsoever. In this way, Furman was not consistent in his confessional Calvinism. Furman emphasized the satisfaction of justice and the honor paid to God the Moral

8. Furman, "Oration, Delivered at the Charleston Orphan-House," 349.

9. Furman, "Richard Furman to Gabriel Gerald."

10. Chapter 8 of *The Charleston Confession* does in fact mention that God "upholdeth and governeth all things," but this is simply to articulate a doctrine of providence. It is not with regard to any soteriological framework (*Charleston Confession*, 8.2).

11. *Charleston Confession of Faith*, 6.5, 11.1, 11.5.

12. *Charleston Confession of Faith*, 6.1.

13. *Charleston Confession of Faith*, 19.5.

14. *Charleston Confession of Faith*, 8.3, 8.5, 8.6.

Governor rather than the value of Christ's sufferings and the debt paid to God the Creditor. As a result, he had little use for commercial imagery, even though this kind of imagery was found in *The Charleston Confession*.

Furman did utilize commercial tropes on rare occasions. However, these were only in private letters or in citations of Scripture, and never extensively.[15] Like so many of his contemporaries, Furman did not prefer a commercialized atonement. But this only begs the question: why exactly did Furman overshadow certain prominent confessional themes in order to accentuate others? Moreover, if he was willing to sparingly entertain commercial language, why did these themes not appear regularly in his sermons or treatises? Furman's inconsistency with *The Charleston Confession* and with himself indicates that he was subject to the *zeitgeist* of his revolutionary age, when governmental and even royal language was adopted from the culture around him in order to depict Christ's work. This is part of what Malcolm B. Yarnell III refers to as "Furman's constitutionalism" or his willingness to view the doctrine of Providence in terms of governmental or constitutional power.[16] While this kind of contextualization made him very effective as a leader and as a preacher, it also compelled him to neglect other significant themes in his discussion of the work of Christ. The fact that Furman never detailed his reasoning for this neglect and never explicitly rejected the use of commercial themes is a puzzling piece to his doctrine of atonement.

Another weakness in Richard Furman's doctrine of atonement is his reticence to explain how certain ideas were congruent with others in his brand of moral governmental atonement. For example, in the New Divinity model, Edwardseans did not recognize a fundamental unity between the atonement and the act of salvation because they believed this safeguarded the sovereignty of God's pardoning grace. William B. Johnson explicitly denied such a unity.[17] The atonement is not a saving atonement in itself. According to this scheme, if the sufferings of Christ could be distributed, transferred, or monetized in any way, the grace of God would be eviscerated. One of the primary theological differences between Furman and men such as Johnson and Maxcy on the doctrine of the atonement was that the latter denied any real connection between the atonement and the actual act of pardon. For example, Maxcy upheld the doctrine of substitution, but believed that the "atonement is a substitute for punishments" and not for

---

15. Richard Furman Papers, Acc. 1960–016 [Box #1, Folder #11, 34], Special Collections and Archives, Furman University, Greenville, S.C.; Furman, "Constitution and Order of the Christian Church," 282.

16. Yarnell, "Early American Political Theology," 72.

17. Johnson, "Love Characteristic of the Deity," 60.

actual people.[18] Other New Divinity men redefined certain doctrines to work around this soteriological divide. John Smalley, a disciple of Jonathan Edwards's student Joseph Bellamy, affirmed the idea of imputation, but insisted that Christ's righteousness is not "so imputed to them as to become, to all intents and purposes, their own righteousness."[19] In other words, it is not reckoned to a sinner's personal account, but nevertheless an atonement made on their behalf.

Because the moral governmental atonement is not a literal payment of a debt or a transfer of righteousness, New Divinity men were not interested in the worth or value of Christ's death. In fact, in their view, the atonement itself had no intrinsic value in any measurable sense. Its ultimate purpose was to uphold the honor of God's justice in such a way that God's subsequent pardon of sinners could be completely free. Therefore, they conceived of Christ's atonement not as the actual punishment under the law, but as an act of public suffering equivalent to the damnation of sinners in hell whereby God manifested his displeasure with sin, vindicated his moral governance, and made sovereign grace possible. As Samuel Hopkins explained, Christ "suffers the evil which the law threatens for sin, or a complete equivalent, so as fully to answer the end of the threatening of the law, and all the purposes of moral government, consistent with the pardon of the sinner, as much as if the curse had been executed on the transgressor."[20] In his anthology of Edwardsean works on the atonement (which includes Jonathan Maxcy), Edwards Amasa Park explains, "The atonement is not made, then, by executing the literal penalty of the law, but in some other way, equally advantageous to the honor of the law, and satisfactory to its main spirit and aim."[21] In the Edwardsean scheme, Christ does not endure the literal penalty under the law, but instead suffers amoral equivalent to what would be experienced under the law so that God can freely pardon sinners. What is important is not the exaction of the law itself, but its honor. This is the sense in which most moral governmentalists understood terms such as honor and pardon. But this is not necessarily how Richard Furman used them.

Even though Johnson and Maxcy maintained a separation between the atonement and salvation, Furman did not make a hard division. However, oddly enough, Furman never explained how he was able to reconcile a moral governmental atonement with a unity between atonement and salvation.

18. Maxcy, "Discourse, Designed to Explain the Doctrine of Atonement. In Two Parts, Part II," 70.

19. Smalley, "Justification Through Christ, An Act of Free Grace," 55.

20. Samuel Hopkins, cited in "Introductory Essay," in Park, *Atonement*, lii.

21. Park, *Atonement*, lxxv.

Furman too desired to emphasize the freeness of God's pardoning grace. His un-commercialized, moral governmental atonement was an attempt to accentuate the sovereignty of the Moral Governor in salvation. But he did not safeguard divine sovereignty by separating the atonement from salvation in the way that the New Divinity did. There was a real connection in the Furmanian scheme. For instance, Furman preached that the "righteousness of the Son of God is imputed to those who believe in him" and compared such imputed righteousness to the wearing of a robe.[22] Unlike the New Divinity, Furman clearly defined imputation in the traditional Calvinist frame, as something done personally to each believer. In other words, Christ's righteousness is individually distributed to sinners upon faith.

Secondly, Furman never spoke of Christ's death in terms of an equivalence, but as something performed under the law itself. For example, Furman preached "the fullness of that satisfaction [Christ] has rendered to its penal demands, by suffering the punishment due to sin."[23] Christ did not uphold the integrity of the law and the Moral Governor by a mere public display of suffering; he actually received the penalty of the law. This is another way that the atonement is united to the act of salvation.

Lastly, Furman traversed the atonement-salvation divide with the idea of application. In the New Divinity scheme, the atonement isn't something done to the believer so much as it is something done for God the Moral Governor. It is not applied so much as it becomes the object of faith. However, for Richard Furman, the atonement was something done *to* believers and *for* the Moral Governor. In addition to honoring the Lawgiver, the goal of the atonement is that believers would be "receiving an application of the Savior's benefits; which it is easy for a God of all power and grace to make, by his Holy Spirit to their souls." In this, Christ is "applying to them the blessings of his obedience, atonement, intercession and renewing grace, to reconcile them to God."[24] While dispensing with commutative justice, the Furmanian atonement upholds both distributive and general justice, personally applying the righteous "benefits" of the crucified Christ to believers and maintaining the character of the Moral Governor. Rather than separate the atonement from pardon, Furman attempted to uphold the sovereignty of God's pardoning grace by insisting that Christ's work under the law could be fully accounted to and applied to sinners in faith, but not in such a way that God's grace could be counted or monetized.

---

22. Furman, "Royal Marriage Feast," 471.
23. Furman, On Growth in Grace," 553.
24. Furman, "Of Infant Salvation," 597.

However, despite his attempt to combine elements of traditional and moderate Calvinism, the weakness of Furman's moral government view of the atonement stems from his definition of pardon. It would seem that, in retaining the idea of imputation and Christ's death under the law and the application of the atonement, Furman committed the same alleged errors that most moral governmentalists were attempting to avoid, namely that distributed righteousness and fully-paid penalties undermine grace and individual responsibility. This was Jonathan Edwards Jr.'s primary critique of commutative and distributive justice. According to Edwards Jr., none "will pretend that commutative justice is satisfied by Christ; for the controversy between God and the sinner is not concerning property. Nor is distributive justice satisfied. If it were, there would be no more grace in the discharge of the sinner, than there is in the discharge of a criminal, when he hath endured the full punishment to which, according to law, he hath been condemned."[25] In other words, grace becomes something to be claimed and not something for which to ask in faith. In this way, it seems as if Richard Furman attempted to have his theological cake and to eat it, too. He retained both distributive and general justice. However, if Furman was relentlessly committed to the "sovereign mercy" and the "free pardon" of the Moral Governor, and yet he also insisted that Christ already paid the full penalty of the law of those sinners predestined to believe, in what way can the Moral Governor be said to "pardon" sinners when they have already been legally exonerated?[26] According to Furman's view of the atonement, Christ not only honors the law, but fully meets all of its "demands" for those who would believe. In this way, according to the traditional moral governmental scheme, faith is not so much a request for free pardon from the Moral Governor as it is a claim for what is owed. At the very least, Furman did not explain the nature of the Moral Governor's pardon. At the very worst, Furman's version of moral governmental atonement does not solve the problems which many of his New Divinity friends were trying to address in the traditional penal substitutionary view. For Maxcy and Johnson, the actual act of pardon occurred upon faith, not at the cross. For Furman, as has been shown, pardon was executed in the atonement itself, by death of Christ. Time and again, Furman associated pardon and blood inside his tripartite scheme.[27] Therefore, Furman believed that pardon was lawfully applied by Christ and the Holy Spirit and not freely bestowed by a sovereign

---

25. Edwards, "Inferences and Reflections," in Park, *Atonement*, 37.
26. Furman, "Royal Marriage Feast," 470.
27. Furman, "On Growth in Grace," 554; Furman, "On the Communion of Saints," 564.

God, something that was unacceptable to most who held to the moral governmental scheme. In trying to engineer a synthesis of moral governmental and penal substitutionary models, Furman surrendered a degree of freedom from the Moral Governor in pardoning sinners, the very thing he prized most. Richard Furman's greatest strength in his doctrine of atonement was his ability to blend different themes and views, however, this sometimes became a weakness.

Substitution and Penalty

Richard Furman's penal substitutionary framework compromised a bit of his moral governmental project. Conversely, his moral governmental commitments altered his penal substitutionary framework, specifically his view of substitution. In what way can Richard Furman's doctrine of atonement be penal substitutionary if indeed he never used the word "substitution" to describe the atonement? As shown, Furman certainly operated within a substitutionary framework, utilizing concepts like propitiation and insisting that Christ's atonement was "wrought out for us" and made "for his redeemed."[28] According to his covenant theology, Furman certainly viewed Christ as a "representative" and "public head."[29] However, representation and substitution are not theologically synonymous.

Did Richard Furman merely de-emphasize the idea of substitution in favor of a moral governmental frame? Or was his silence on substitution an indication that he rejected it on some level? As a conciliatory, moderate Calvinist, Furman's theology begs these kinds of questions. As shown, Furman's view does not align with what Cooley and Sweeney have called a *"non-distributive* form of penal substitution" because he clearly upheld the traditional doctrine of imputation.[30] Furman made much of the earthly obedience of Christ and its righteous benefit for sinners. Furman also affirmed the idea of penalty in Christ's work. The divine law has "penal demands" which are met by Christ's atoning death.[31] Furman understood that "the claims of justice demand" the death of the wicked as much as they

---

28. Furman, "Royal Marriage Feast," 470; Furman, "Of Growth in Grace," 553.

29. Furman, "Of Infant Salvation," 594.

30. Cooley and Sweeney, "Edwardseans and the Atonement," 122. Cooley and Sweeney explain, "Instead of Christ being the substitute victim for man, Christ's sufferings are substituted for man's punishment. Instead of the atonement being distributed to each one of God's elect individually, it is construed as a collective satisfaction for all who believe" (122).

31. Furman, "On Growth in Grace," 553.

require Christ to uphold the honor of the Moral Governor in salvation.[32] In fact, Furman interpreted the penalty of the law through the lens of God's moral government. "Death was threatened as the punishment of sin," Furman insisted, "when the Great Creator, and Moral Governor, gave his first law to man: And its introduction, continuance, and power, afford convincing proof of the rebellion, guilt, and general depravity of the human race."[33]

In some way, Furman understood Christ to die *for* sinners on their behalf. As the typological fulfillment of the Passover Lamb in Exodus, Christ's role was to "fulfill that sacred, typical institution in the sacrifice of himself."[34] In this sense, Furman believed that Christ died instead of believers. Christ's death was a "propitiatory sacrifice" wherein Christ met the penal demands of justice rather than the sinner in hell.[35] This view is consistent with what Gustaf Aulen identified as the dominant Protestant teaching after the Reformation. Aulen explained, "The idea of God which underlies it is, above all, that of a Justice which imposes its law and demands satisfaction; only within these limits is the Divine Love allowed to operate."[36] Furman fit this Protestant mold, but in a moral governmental context. To Furman, the atonement must always be "consistent with his glorious perfections and righteous government."[37] In this way, Furman meets Gathercole's criteria for a substitutionary atonement, or "Christ's death in our place, instead of us."[38] In Furman's view, Christ's death is an atonement for sin which satisfies divine justice and meets the law's "penal demands" such that believers do not meet those demands in judgment. He dies *instead of* sinners and *for* sinners. Furman was careful not to say that Christ "pays" the penalty of the law. He is much more concerned with justice than payment, and this qualifies his idea of substitution.

Richard Furman affirmed a penal substitutionary atonement in which Christ died in the place of sinners, but not directly. In Gathercole's words, Christ died "instead of" sinners, but not in a *quid pro quo* sense. In other words, Furman did not affirm an "exchange" of righteousness or penalty in a commutative brand of justice. He never references the atonement in this manner. On a rare occasion, Furman described Christ's role as the second Adam as a "transaction" in his exegesis of Romans 5, but he did not elaborate

32. Furman, "Death's Dominion Over Man Considered," 233.
33. Furman, "Death's Dominion Over Man Considered," 232–33.
34. Furman, "Rewards of Grace," 320.
35. Furman, "Conversion Essential to Salvation," 433.
36. Aulen, *Christus Victor*, 130.
37. Furman, "On the Use of Reason in Religion," 529.
38. Gathercole, *Defending Substitution*, 15.

on his meaning.[39] In the same breath, Furman also described the transfer of Adam's guilt to sinners as a "transaction," indicating that this idea did not necessarily denote an exchange, as the sinner gives nothing to Adam. On another rare occasion, Furman preached of the "transactions of judgment" in hell, again demonstrating that Furman did not employ this word to mean an actual exchange, as damned sinners transfer nothing to the Judge.[40]

Nevertheless, while his doctrine of imputation involved Christ's righteousness given personally to the sinner, this was only through the "application" of Christ's work by the Spirit and not in a direct exchange of merit. Furman never entertained the idea that Christ took the individual believer's sin upon himself directly in a soteriological swap of sorts. There is no one-to-one trade. Instead, for example, Furman often utilized the expiatory idea of "removal." Furman defined a "propitiatory sacrifice" as one where "their guilt, through his atonement, is completely removed; and by the act of grace, cast, as it were, into the depths of the sea, to be seen or remembered no more."[41] In another instance, Furman spoke of "the removal of the righteous from their present state of existence."[42] By his obedience and death on the cross, and by its "application," Christ removes the sinner's guilt and imputes his own righteousness to the believer. However, he does not exchange guilt for righteousness. Instead, by his atoning work, he removes guilt and applies righteousness. In so doing, Christ satisfies the demands of the law in a manner consistent with God's moral government. Richard Furman's substitutionary atonement is an *indirect* substitutionary atonement in the sense that no *quid pro quo* exchange of merit takes place, but the merits are nevertheless applied and removed.

When Furman applauded the "fixed Calvinist" theology of his predecessor Oliver Hart at Hart's funeral, Furman emphasized the idea of efficacy: "The doctrines of free, efficacious grace, were precious to him; Christ Jesus, and him crucified, in the perfection of his righteousness, the merit of his death, the prevalence of his intercession, and efficacy of his grace, was the foundation of his hope, the source of his joy, and the delightful theme of his preaching."[43] Whether or not Oliver Hart made such careful distinctions as his successor, Furman nevertheless believed that the efficacy of grace, not necessarily its exchange, was the most important part of the

39. Furman, "Of Infant Salvation," 592.

40. Manuscript, sermon on Death, Psalm 39:4, undated, Richard Furman Papers, Acc. 1960–016 [Series II, Box #3, #3], Special Collections and Archives, Furman University, Greenville, S.C.

41. Furman, "Conversion Essential to Salvation," 433.

42. Furman, "Death's Dominion Over Man Considered," 233.

43. Furman, "Rewards of Grace," 337.

atonement. Furman was not the only South Carolina Baptist to hold this view. An indirect substitution view was also held by Furman's protégé William T. Brantly. Brantly advocated against a traditional exchange theory because, in his words, "if. . .the Substitute, endured all that they were liable to endure, how can they be liable, even anterior to faith and repentance? Here is a difficulty which we confess ourselves unable to dispose of, without modifying the idea of substitution."[44] In other words, the traditional, direct notion of substitution undermined Christian responsibility. Furman circumvented this problem with the idea of application. While Furman's exact purposes for such an indirect view cannot be fully known, he clearly did so to highlight the sovereignty of grace, and he also believed that the idea of the atonement's "application" was sufficient to safeguard Christian responsibility. Richard Furman's doctrine of penal substitution, like his moral governmental theory, did not necessarily reflect the views of others who held to the same framework. Nevertheless, Furman remained within the bounds of a penal substitutionary atonement to justify the label itself, albeit in a less conventional way.

A Reasonable Synthesis?

Although the differences between the Grotian and Edwardsean moral governmental theories of the atonement have been outlined, Millard Erickson's critique of Hugo Grotius's view is equally valid for that of the New Divinity. While recognizing "an objective element" in the moral governmental theory, Erickson insists,

> But in the main, the governmental theory is a subjective theory of the atonement—the chief impact was on human beings. Christ's suffering serves as a deterrent to sin by impressing on us the gravity of sin. As we then turn from sin, we can be forgiven. The need for us to be punished has been eliminated, and yet, at the same time, moral government and the authority of the law have been upheld. Thus, in the long run, the chief impact of the atonement is on humans.[45]

Erickson's critique is indeed consistent with the public nature of sin and salvation in the moral governmental view. Just as sin publicly offends the Moral Governor, the atonement is a public vindication before his moral universe

---

44. Brantly, "Difficulties Attending the Discussion of the Doctrine of the Atonement," 338.

45. Erickson, *Christian Theology*, 722.

wherein God demonstrates the heinousness of sin and the goodness of the law. As a result, many, including Erickson and Garrett Jr., believe that the governmental view is a subjective theory of the atonement at its core.[46]

Richard Furman's version of moral governmental theory, here called "governmental substitution," is not adequately reflected by Erickson's critique. While Furman believed that the aim of the atonement was the "chief happiness" of God's creatures and the public honor of God, his insistence upon the fulfillment of divine justice by the law ensured that his overall view was objectively oriented toward God as much as it was subjectively oriented toward human beings.[47] The chief effect of the atonement is equally upon the Creator and his creatures. In other words, it was not simply for the spectators in God's moral universe and it was not a mere deterrent to bad behavior; it was also for the Moral Governor himself. Sin is not just a societal ill; it is inherently evil. Furman believed that sin "dishonors God by the evil contained in itself."[48] In addition to the good of his moral universe, a holy God must also punish sin for its own sake and his. In Furman's view, the death of Christ is performed under the law. It is not an "equivalent" to God's judgment nor is it simply a penal example of God's displeasure with sin. The cross is God's *real* judgment of sin upon his own Son.

To satisfy divine justice and to satisfy the law's penalty are one and the same in Richard Furman's view. This is what Furman meant when he spoke of Christ rendering satisfaction to the law's "penal demands." Christ is "suffering the punishment due to sin, where he has made a complete atonement for his redeemed."[49] Christ gave what was due to objective justice by dying under the law itself, not by simply honoring the law by a public display of subjective suffering. In the words of Michael Horton, "the cross not only *demonstrates* God's justice (as if it took the cruel death of the Son of God to offer us merely an object lesson) but *fulfills* God's justice."[50] The Furmanian atonement is both real and symbolic justice. It demonstrates justice, displays God's glory, and discharges the righteous demands of God's law.

Richard Furman's governmental substitution theory is a reasonable synthesis of penal substitutionary and moral governmental views because it seeks to honor divine justice by the law itself. However, it also gives due consideration to God's concern for his moral universe and the happiness of his subjects, or as Furman explained, "for your own true happiness; for

---

46. Garrett, *Systematic Theology*, 26–27.
47. Furman, "Conversion Essential to Salvation," 425.
48. Furman, "On Covetousness," 578.
49. Furman, "On Growth in Grace," 553.
50. Horton, *Christian Faith*, 515.

the honor of God."[51] Furman engineered a theory of the atonement which gave equal weight to both of these axioms: the chief good of the moral universe and the greatest honor to the Moral Governor. Furman's governmental substitution model is both objective and subjective, focused upon both God and those he is redeeming in Christ. It's "chief impact" is really upon both. Furman believed that "God is the supporter of justice," and that the display of divine justice be executed for God's glory and the good of his creation.[52] Richard Furman attempted to mold his doctrine of atonement around divine honor and human happiness. "Salvation is of God alone," Furman explained,

> Of his free, unmerited grace. And this we must acknowledge, whether we contemplate it in its origin, the Eternal Council of Divine wisdom, love, and mercy, which has, for lost man, provided a Savior, in the rich blessings of grace and glory it bestows; or in that sovereign efficacy, by which grace arrests and subdues, careless, rebellious sinners, who, in a moral sense, are, by nature, dead in trespasses and sins. But though this work is the Lord's, and the unrivalled glory belongs to him, there is yet something for his servants to perform, as instruments and means in his hands, for accomplishing his merciful purposes. Having themselves, tasted that he is gracious, they are directed to invite others, to come and be partakers, with them, of the same excellent blessings.[53]

While Furman's doctrine of atonement certainly had its weaknesses, his tailored concept of substitution combined with his unique definition of "pardon" were designed to highlight divine sovereignty and the free nature of divine grace in a way that did not diminish the honor and authority of divine justice. Furman's project was equally about law and love. The result is "so that a strict and sacred regard be preserved to the authority and honor of Christ, to the truths he has revealed, the commands he has delivered, and the ordinances he has instituted."[54] By taking into account the public nature of sin and salvation and balancing sovereign grace with strict justice, Richard Furman was able to co-opt many of the strengths of moral governmental theory and blend them with a penal substitutionary frame.
Conclusion

---

51. Furman, "On the Use of Reason in Religion," 527.
52. Furman, "America's Deliverance of Duty," 400.
53. Furman, "Royal Marriage Feast," 466.
54. Furman, "On the Communion of Saints," 571.

Following Furman's death, the editor of the *Charleston Mercury* called him "a man of no common character." He then eulogized the Charleston pastor and depicted his legacy as few others could: "Dr. Furman united a simple, unaffected dignity, and a countenance indicating a strong and comprehensive intellect . . . and a humility which may be termed sublime. He added the manners of a gentleman rectified and refined by the principles of the Christian, the love, reverence and respect which were always paid him by all classes of people."[55] Richard Furman embodied both piety and authority, grace and lawfulness. Therefore, in some ways, his doctrine of atonement exhibited the same principles as his own life. While Furman was not a systematic theologian in the mold of a John Gill or an Andrew Fuller, and while his doctrine of atonement contained certain peculiarities for his era, by no means does this mean that his theology was homespun or incoherent. Possessing "such progress as would have ranked him among men of the first intelligence in any country," Furman knew exactly what he believed and why.[56] His ideas and his doctrines were well-developed and purposeful. Whatever tension or seeming ambiguities that existed in his doctrine of atonement were not due to a lack of theological acumen or attention to detail; these were complexities which Furman intentionally brought together for the sake of a robust gospel.

Furman, the inaugural president of the Triennial Convention, was not only one of the greatest Baptist leaders for his era; he was also a first-rate thinker. His doctrine of atonement is a window in the mind of a revolutionary Baptist who bridged the gap between confessional Calvinism and New Divinity theology, an unlikely combination in many respects. For this reason, Furman gives us better insight into the pursuits and the values of his age. Furman clothed his evangelical Calvinism in modern concepts and shied away from the language of "limited atonement" for the sake of converting the lost. For this reason, W. Wiley Richards's description of Furman as a "moderate" Calvinist is appropriate, especially in his doctrine of atonement.[57] Perhaps by better understanding the moderate Calvinist mind of Richard Furman, the pastor of First Baptist Church of Charleston who was converted by Separate Baptists, labels such as "Charleston" and "Sandy Creek" will no longer prove as dichotomous as they once appeared. Moreover, Furman also compels more nuance and precision when defining Calvinism in the early Baptist South. As Furman demonstrates, not all Calvinists believed the same things about the nature and extent of God's grace.

55. In Rogers, *Richard Furman*, 256.
56. Armitage, "Dr. Richard Furman," 8.
57. Richards, *Winds of Doctrines*, 18.

CRITICAL ANALYSIS OF FURMAN'S DOCTRINE OF ATONEMENT   103

However, Richard Furman is not simply a lesson in history. His doctrine of atonement contains a few lessons of its own. According to Daniel W. Cooley and Douglas A. Sweeney, "Adaptation was a hallmark of Jonathan Edwards and his followers. This willingness to adapt often placed them at the center of controversy. The followers of Edwards sought to promote a version of Reformed theology that they thought would best advance the cause of religion and revival in New England."[58] Richard Furman, although not a New England theologian and not a thoroughgoing New Divinity man, was likewise skilled in theological adaptation. In this, he had much in common with his friends William B. Johnson and Jonathan Maxcy. Many Southern Baptists were willing to adapt their doctrine of atonement in different ways.

Furman was not a theological chameleon who simply took on the soteriological form of his surroundings. Instead, he was an eclectic theologian willing to deliver the gospel in modern speech. As a confessional Calvinist, Furman never forsook the doctrines of *The Charleston Confession*. However, he was not afraid to utilize the language and concepts of his era to better contextualize and elucidate the teachings of the Bible. He was, in some sense, all things to all people. From his usage of Edwardsean concepts to his affinity for governmental and kingly language, Furman drew from non-Baptist cultural sources to promote a very ecumenical message of salvation. On the other hand, Furman also demonstrates the limits of any human framework. While he did not abandon confessional theology, he downplayed commercial themes in order to suit his version of the atonement. Even though Furman eschewed "systems," he did in fact have a system of his own, albeit an eclectic one.

The idea that God is not a Creditor seeking payment, but a sovereign Moral Governor who reigns over his moral universe, permeated almost every aspect of Furman's soteriology and even his doctrine of providence. Furman did not believe this to be an unbiblical way of thinking. His doctrine of atonement was the centerpiece of his doctrine of salvation, and Furman utilized a host of moral governmental themes in order to accentuate the sovereignty of God's grace and the honor and authority of the law. He upheld a blend of penal substitutionary and moral governmental views. He achieved this by de-emphasizing the commercial nature of the atonement, depicting the atonement as a free pardon by a gracious Moral Governor, and by stressing that the atonement was something which required "application" in order to effect salvation. Richard Furman's governmental substitutionary atonement is an excellent example to the Baptist community that multiple "theories" of the atonement are not always mutually exclusive, and they

---

58. Cooley and Sweeney, "Edwardseans and the Atonement," 109.

can often be partially blended, but not without sacrificing certain aspects of each. Furman lived with the theological tension between the penal substitutionary and moral governmental views. Furman's project of bringing together multiple views of the atonement is proof that Baptist theologians are not necessarily required to first choose between systematic "theories" of the atonement, but should rather seek after the truths and themes of Scripture and compose their doctrine of atonement accordingly.

Bibliography

Ahlstrom, Sydney E. *A Religious History of the American People*. 2nd ed. New Haven, CT: Yale University Press, 2004.
Allen, David. *The Extent of the Atonement: A Historical and Critical Review*. Nashville: B&H Academic, 2016.
Anderson, Courtney. *To the Golden Shore: The Life of Adoniram Judson*. Valley Forge, PA: Judson, 1987.
Armitage, Thomas. "Dr. Richard Furman." In *A History of the Baptists; Traced by their Vital Principles and Practices, from the Time of Our Lord and Saviour Jesus Christ to the Year 1889*, 812–13. New York: Bryan, Taylor, & Co., 1889.
Bailyn, Bernard. *The Ideological Origins of the American Revolution*. Cambridge, MA: Harvard University Press, 1967.
Baker, J. Wayne. *Heinrich Bullinger and the Covenant*. Athens, OH: Ohio University Press, 1980.
Baker, Robert A., and Craven, Paul J., Jr. *Adventure in Faith: The First 300 Years of First Baptist Church, Charleston, South Carolina*. Nashville: Broadman, 1982.
Ball, John H., III. *Chronicling the Soul's Windings: Thomas Hooker and His Morphology of Conversion*. Lanham, MD: University Press of America, 1992.
Bercovitch, Sacvan. *The American Jeremiad*. Madison: University of Wisconsin Press, 1978.
Berkhof, Louis. *Systematic Theology*. Carlisle, PA: Banner of Truth Trust, 2012.
Botsford, Edmund. *Memoirs of Edmund Botsford*. Edited by Charles D. Mallary. Springfield, MO: Particular Baptist Press, 2004.
Boyce, James Petigru. *Abstract of Systematic Theology*. Charleston, SC: den Dulk Christian Foundation, 1887.
———. *Three Changes in Theological Institutions*. Greenville, SC: C. J. Elford's Book and Job Press, 1856.
Brantly, William T. "Extracts from Dr. W. T. Brantly's Sermon Delivered in 1825." In *The Life and Works of Dr. Richard Furman, D.D.*, edited by G. William Foster Jr., 211–25. Harrisonburg, VA: Sprinkle, 2004.
———. "Original Anecdotes of Dr. Rush." *The Christian Index* (October 6, 1832).
———. *The Saint's Repose in Death. A Sermon Delivered on the Death of Richard Furman, D. D. Late Pastor of the Baptist Church, Charleston, S. C.* Charleston, SC: W. Riley, 1825.
———. "Solitary Hours." *The Christian Index* 19 (February 1831).

———. *Themes for Meditation, Enlarged in Several Sermons, Doctrinal and Practical.* Philadelphia: Sherman, 1837.

Brewster, Paul. *Andrew Fuller: Model Pastor-Theologian.* Nashville: B&H, 2010.

Calamy, Edmund. *Two Solemne Covenants Made between God and Man: viz. The Covenant of Works, and the Covenant of Grace.* London: Thomas Banks, 1647.

Caldwell, Robert W., III. *Theologies of the American Revivalists: From Whitefield to Finney.* Downers Grove, IL: InterVarsity, 2017.

Chun, Chris. *The Legacy of Jonathan Edwards in the Theology of Andrew Fuller.* Leiden: Brill, 2012.

Chute, Anthony L., et al., eds. *The Baptist Story: From English Sect to Global Movement.* Nashville: B&H Academic, 2015.

Clipsham, E. F. "Andrew Fuller and Fullerism: A Study in Evangelical Calvinism." *Baptist Quarterly* 20 (1964) 99–114.

Conforti, Joseph A. *Samuel Hopkins and the New Divinity Movement: Calvinism and Reform in New England between the Great Awakenings.* Eugene, OR: Wipf & Stock, 1981.

Cook, Harvey T. *A Biography of Richard Furman.* Greenville, SC: Baptist Courier Job Rooms, 1913.

Cooley, Daniel W., and Sweeney, Douglas A. "The Edwardseans and the Atonement." In *A New Divinity: Transatlantic Reformed Evangelical Debates during the Long Eighteenth Century,* edited by Mark Jones and Michael A. G. Haykin, 109–25. Gottingen: Vandenhoeck & Ruprecht, 2018.

Crisp, Oliver D. "The Moral Government of God: Jonathan Edwards and Joseph Bellamy on the Atonement." In *After Jonathan Edwards: The Courses of the New England Theology,* edited by Oliver D. Crisp and Douglas A. Sweeney, 78–90. New York: Oxford University Press, 2012.

———. "Non-Penal Substitution." *International Journal of Systematic Theology* 9 (2007) 415–33.

———. "Penal Non-Substitution." *Journal of Theological Studies* 59 (2008) 140–68.

Dagg, John L. *Manual of Theology.* Berryville, VA: Hess, 1998.

Denault, Pascal. *The Distinctiveness of Baptist Covenant Theology: A Comparison between Seventeenth-Century Particular Baptist and Paedobaptist Federalism.* Birmingham, AL: Solid Ground Christian, 2013.

Dwight, Timothy. *Theology; Explained and Defended in a Series of Sermons, Vol. 2.* New Haven, CT: T. Dwight & Son, 1839.

Edwards, Jonathan. *The Works of Jonathan Edwards, Volume 1: Freedom of the Will.* New Haven, CT: Yale University Press, 1957.

———. *The Works of Jonathan Edwards, Volume 16: Letters and Personal Writings.* New Haven, CT: Yale University Press, 1988.

Fitzmier, John R. *New England's Moral Legislator: Timothy Dwight, 1752–1817.* Bloomington: Indiana University Press, 1998.

Foster, William G., Jr. "Preface." In *The Life and Works of Dr. Richard Furman, D.D.,* edited by G. William Foster Jr., xi–xviii. Harrisonburg, VA: Sprinkle, 2004.

Fuller, Andrew. *The Complete Works of the Rev. Andrew Fuller, Vol. 1–3.* Harrisonburg, VA: Sprinkle, 1988.

———. "To Timothy Dwight." In *The Armies of the Lamb: The Spirituality of Andrew Fuller,* edited by Michael A. G. Haykin, 199–201. Dundas, Ontario: Joshua, 2001.

Bibliography

Furman, Richard. "Address of the Convention." In *The Life and Works of Dr. Richard Furman, D.D.*, edited by G. William Foster Jr., 443–52. Harrisonburg, VA: Sprinkle, 2004.

———. "America's Deliverance and Duty. A Sermon on the Anniversary of American Independence, July 4, 1802." In *The Life and Works of Dr. Richard Furman, D.D.*, edited by G. William Foster Jr., 389–408. Harrisonburg, VA: Sprinkle, 2004.

———. "Conversion Essential to Salvation." In *The Life and Works of Dr. Richard Furman, D.D.*, edited by G. William Foster Jr., 419–22. Harrisonburg, VA: Sprinkle, 2004.

———. *Exposition of the Views of the Baptists Relative to the Coloured Population of the United States in Communication to the Governor of South Carolina*. Ithaca, NY: Cornell University Library, 1823.

———. "Humble Submission to Divine Sovereignty. The Duty of a Bereaved Nation: A Sermon, Occasioned by the Death of His Excellency General George Washington." In *The Life and Works of Dr. Richard Furman, D.D.*, edited by G. William Foster Jr., 365–87. Harrisonburg, VA: Sprinkle, 2004.

———. "Hymn II." In *Life and Works of Dr. Richard Furman, D.D.*, edited by G. William Foster Jr., 410. Harrisonburg, VA: Sprinkle, 2004.

———. "A Letter from Dr. Furman of Charleston, to Dr. Rippon of London, Regarding a Camp Meeting He Attended." In *The Life and Works of Dr. Richard Furman, D.D.*, edited by G. William Foster Jr., 413–17. Harrisonburg, VA: Sprinkle, 2004.

———. Letter to Oliver Hart. July 25, 1790. Richard Furman Papers. James B. Duke Library, Furman University, Greenville, SC.

———. "Of Infant Salvation." In *The Life and Works of Dr. Richard Furman, D.D.*, edited by G. William Foster Jr., 585–602. Harrisonburg, VA: Sprinkle, 2004.

———. "On the Analogy between the Dispensation of Grace by the Gospel, and a Royal Marriage Feast." In *The Life and Works of Dr. Richard Furman, D.D.*, edited by G. William Foster Jr., 465–81. Harrisonburg, VA: Sprinkle, 2004.

———. "On the Communion of Saints." In *The Life and Works of Dr. Richard Furman, D.D.*, edited by G. William Foster Jr., 563–73. Harrisonburg, VA: Sprinkle, 2004.

———. "On the Constitution and Order of the Christian Church." In *The Life and Works of Dr. Richard Furman, D.D.*, edited by G. William Foster Jr., 257–86. Harrisonburg, VA: Sprinkle, 2004.

———. "On Covetousness." In *The Life and Works of Dr. Richard Furman, D.D.*, edited by G. William Foster Jr., 575–84. Harrisonburg, VA: Sprinkle, 2004.

———. "On the Duty of Churches to Provide for the Instruction and Improvement of Persons Called by Them to the Ministry; Previous to Their Entering on the Work." In *The Life and Works of Dr. Richard Furman, D.D.*, edited by G. William Foster Jr., 505–17. Harrisonburg, VA: Sprinkle, 2004.

———. "On Growth in Grace." In *The Life and Works of Dr. Richard Furman, D.D.*, edited by G. William Foster Jr., 551–62. Harrisonburg, VA: Sprinkle, 2004.

———. "On the Languishing State of Religion in the Southern States." In *The Life and Works of Dr. Richard Furman, D.D.*, edited by G. William Foster Jr., 533–43. Harrisonburg, VA: Sprinkle, 2004.

———. "On the Relation the Children of Church Members Bear to the Church, and the Duties Arising from That Relation." In *The Life and Works of Dr. Richard Furman, D.D.*, edited by G. William Foster Jr., 487–504. Harrisonburg, VA: Sprinkle, 2004.

———. "On Religious and Civil Duties." In *The Life and Works of Dr. Richard Furman, D.D.*, edited by G. William Foster Jr., 545–49. Harrisonburg, VA: Sprinkle, 2004.

———. "On the Use of Reason in Religion." In *The Life and Works of Dr. Richard Furman, D.D.*, edited by G. William Foster Jr., 519–32. Harrisonburg, VA: Sprinkle, 2004.

———. "An Oration, Delivered at the Charleston Orphan-House." In *The Life and Works of Dr. Richard Furman, D.D.*, edited by G. William Foster Jr., 343–63. Harrisonburg, VA: Sprinkle, 2004.

———. "Rewards of Grace Conferred on Christ's Faithful People: A Sermon, Occasioned by the Decease of the Rev. Oliver Hart, A.M." In *The Life and Works of Dr. Richard Furman, D.D.*, edited by G. William Foster Jr., 317–41. Harrisonburg, VA: Sprinkle, 2004.

———. "Richard Furman to Gabriel Gerald." Richard Furman Papers, Acc. 1960-016 [Box #1, Folder #11], Special Collections and Archives, Furman University, Greenville, SC.

———. "Saints in Heavenly Rest." 1802. Richard Furman Papers. James B. Duke Library, Furman University, Greenville, SC.

———. "Sketch of the Life of the Rev. Edm'd Botsford, A.M." In *The Life and Works of Dr. Richard Furman, D.D.*, edited by G. William Foster Jr., 453–63. Harrisonburg, VA: Sprinkle, 2004.

———. "Unity and Peace." In *The Life and Works of Dr. Richard Furman, D.D.*, edited by G. William Foster Jr., 287–316. Harrisonburg, VA: Sprinkle, 2004.

Garrett, James Leo, Jr. *Baptist Theology: A Four-Century Study*. Macon, GA: Mercer University Press, 2009.

Gathercole, Simon. *Defending Substitution: An Essay on Atonement in Paul*. Grand Rapids: Baker Academic, 2015.

George, Timothy, and Dockery, David S., eds. *Baptist Theologians*. Nashville: Broadman, 1990.

Gibson, David, and Gibson, Jonathan, eds. *From Heaven He Came and Sought Her: Definite Atonement in Historical, Biblical, Theological, and Pastoral Perspective*. Wheaton, IL: Crossway, 2013.

Gillette, A. D., ed. *Minutes of the Philadelphia Baptist Association, from A.D. 1707 to A.D. 1807*. Philadelphia: American Baptist Publication Society, 1851.

Grotius, Hugo. *The Life and Works of Hugo Grotius*. Farmington Hills, MI: Gale, 2010.

Hambrick-Stowe, Charles. "The New England Theology in New England Congregationalism." In *After Jonathan Edwards: The Courses of the New England Theology*, edited by Oliver D. Crisp and Douglas A. Sweeney, 165–77. New York: Oxford University Press, 2012.

Hamilton, S. Mark. "Re-Thinking Atonement in Jonathan Edwards and New England Theology." *Perichoresis* 15 (2017) 85–99.

Hankins, Barry, and Thomas S. Kidd. *Baptists in America: A History*. Oxford: Oxford University Press, 2015.

Hart, Oliver. Letter to Richard Furman. May 30, 1793. Richard Furman Papers. James B. Duke Library, Furman University, Greenville, SC.

Hatch, Nathan O. *The Democratization of American Christianity*. New Haven, CT: Yale University Press, 1991.

Haykin, Michael A. G. "Great Admirers of the Transatlantic Divinity: Some Chapters in the Story of Baptist Edwardsianism." In *After Jonathan Edwards: The Courses *of the New England Theology*, edited by Oliver D. Crisp and Douglas A. Sweeney, 197–207. New York: Oxford University Press, 2012.

Holifield, E. Brooks. *Theology in America: Christian Thought from the Age of the Puritans to the Civil War*. New Haven, CT: Yale University Press, 2003.

Jauhiainen, Peter. "Samuel Hopkins and Hopkinsianism." In *After Jonathan Edwards: The Courses of the New England Theology*, edited by Oliver D. Crisp and Douglas A. Sweeney, 107–17. New York: Oxford University Press, 2012.

Johnson, William B. Letter to James S. Mims, March 25, 1848, William B. Johnson Papers, James B. Duke Library, Furman University, Greenville, SC.

———. "Love Characteristic of the Deity." In *Southern Baptist Sermons on Sovereignty and Responsibility*. Harrisonburg, VA: Sprinkle, 2003.

———. "Richard Furman, D.D." In *Life and Works of Dr. Richard Furman, D.D.* Harrisonburg, VA: Sprinkle, 2004.

Kidd, Thomas S. *The Great Awakening: The Roots of Evangelical Christianity in Colonial America*. New Haven, CT: Yale University Press, 2007.

King, Joe M. *A History of South Carolina Baptists*. Columbia: The General Board of the South Carolina Baptist Convention, 1964.

Knowles, James D. *Memoir of Mrs. Ann H. Judson, Late Missionary to Burmah*, 3rd ed. Boston: Lincoln & Edmands, 1829.

Lynd, Samuel W. *Memoir of the Rev. William Staughton, D.D.* Boston: Lincoln, Edmands & Co., 1834.

Mallary, Charles Dutton. *Memoirs of Elder Jesse Mercer*. New York: Gray, 1844.

Manly, Basil. *Mercy and Judgment: A Discourse, Containing Some Fragments of the History of the Baptist Church in Charleston, S.C.* Providence, RI: Vose, 1837.

Manning, James. Letter to Richard Furman. February 15, 1791. Richard Furman Papers. James B. Duke Library, Furman University, Greenville, SC.

Marsden, George M. "The Quest for the Historical Edwards: The Challenge of Biography." In *Jonathan Edwards at Home and Abroad: Historical Memories, Cultural Movements, Global Horizons*, ed. David W. Kling and Douglas A. Sweeney, 3–15. Columbia: University of South Carolina Press, 2003.

Mercer, Jesse. *Ten Letters, Addressed to the Reverend Cyrus White, in Reference to His Scriptural View of the Atonement*. Washington, GA: The Christian Index News Office, 1830.

Nettles, Thomas J. "Richard Furman." In *Baptist Theologians*, edited by David Dockery and Timothy George, 140–64. Nashville: Broadman, 1990.

Nettles, Tom. "Richard Furman (1755–1825)." In *The Baptists: Key People Involved in Forming a Baptist Identity: Volume Two: Beginnings in America*, 125–152. Fearn, Scotland: Mentor, 2005.

Noll, Mark A. *America's God: From Jonathan Edwards to Abraham Lincoln*. Oxford: Oxford University Press, 2002.

O'Brien, Michael. *Intellectual Life and the American South, 1810–1860*. Chapel Hill: University of North Carolina Press, 2010.

Oliver, Robert W. *History of the English Calvinistic Baptists 1771–1892: From John Gill to C.H. Spurgeon*. Carlisle, PA: Banner of Truth Trust, 2006.

Park, Edwards Amasa, ed. *The Atonement, Discourses and Treatises by Edwards, Smalley, Maxcy, Emmons, Griffin, Burge, and Weeks*. Boston: Congregational Board of Publication, 1859.

———. "New England Theology." *Bibliotheca Sacra* 9(1852) 169–217.

Pendleton, James Madison. *The Atonement of Christ*. Philadelphia: American Baptist Publication Society, 1885.

Pittsley, Jeremy. "Christ's Absolute Determination to Save: Andrew Fuller and Particular Redemption." *Eusebeia* 9 (April 2008) 135–66.

Randall, Ian M., et al., eds. *Baptist Identities: International Studies from the Seventeenth to the Twentieth Centuries*. Paternoster Studies in Baptist History and Thought. Eugene, OR: Wipf & Stock, 2006.

Reynolds, J. Alvin. "The Life and Work of Richard Furman." PhD diss., New Orleans Baptist Theological Seminary, 1962.

Richards, W. Wiley. *Winds of Doctrines: The Origin and Development of Southern Baptist Theology*. Lanham, MD: University Press of America, 1991.

Rogers, James A. *Richard Furman: Life and Legacy*. Macon, GA: Mercer University Press, 2011.

Rudisill, Dorus Paul. *The Doctrine of the Atonement in Jonathan Edwards and His Successors*. New York: Poseidon, 1971.

Sellers, Charles. *The Market Revolution: Jacksonian America, 1815–1846*. New York: Oxford University Press, 1991.

Smith, Craig Bruce. *American Honor: The Creation of the Nation's Ideals during the Revolutionary Era*. Chapel Hill: University of North Carolina Press, 2018.

Smith, Eric C. "Order and Ardor: The Revival Spirituality of Regular Baptist Oliver Hart (1723–1795)." PhD diss., The Southern Baptist Theological Seminary, 2015.

Sweeney, Douglas A. *Nathaniel Taylor, New Haven Theology, and the Legacy of Jonathan Edwards*. New York: Oxford University Press, 2003.

Todd, Obbie Tyler. "Did Jonathan Edwards Help Inspire the Modern Missionary Movement?" In *A Collection of Essays on Jonathan Edwards*, eds. Matthew V. Everhard and Robert L. Boss, 33–48. Fort Worth: JE Society, 2016.

———. "The Influence of Jonathan Edwards on the Missiology and Conversionism of Richard Furman (1755–1825)." *Jonathan Edwards Studies* 7 (2017) 36–54.

Valeri, Mark. *Law and Providence in Joseph Bellamy's New England: The Origins of the New Divinity in Revolutionary America*. Oxford: Oxford University Press, 1994.

Wills, Gregory A. *Democratic Religion: Freedom, Authority, and Church Discipline in the Baptist South (1785–1900)*. Oxford: Oxford University Press, 1997.

———. *The First Baptist Church of Columbia, South Carolina 1809–2002*. Brentwood, TN: Baptist History and Heritage Society, 2003.

———. "The *SBJT* Forum: Overlooked Shapers of Evangelicalism." *The Southern Baptist Journal of Theology* 3 (1999) 87–90.

Wolever, Terry. *The Life of John Gano (1727–1804): Pastor-Evangelist of the Philadelphia Association*. Springfield, MO: Particular Baptist Press, 2012.

Wood, Gordon S. *The Radicalism of the American Revolution*. New York: Vintage, 1993.

Woodson, Hortense. *Giant in the Land: The Life of William B. Johnson, First President of the Southern Baptist Convention (1845–1851)*. Springfield, MO: Particular Baptist Press, 2005.

Wyatt-Brown, Bertram. *Southern Honor: Ethics and Behavior in the Old South*. New York: Oxford University Press, 2007.

Yarnell, Malcolm B., III. "Early American Political Theology." In *First Freedom: The Beginning and End of Religious Liberty*, edited by Jason G. Duesing et al., 49–79. Nashville: B&H Academic, 2016.

Name/Subject Index

Allen, David, 6
atonement
　commercial nature of, 31–32, 91
　complete, 41, 90, 100
　extent, 5
　intent, 5, 49
　limited, 4, 49, 75, 90, 102
　nature, 5
　unlimited, 4, 49
American Revolution, 1, 5, 25, 34, 35
Aulen, Gustaf, 97

Baptists,
　English, 15, 26
　Northern, 16, 26
　Particular, 29
　Regular, 1, 6, 26
　Separate, 1, 6, 25, 102
Bellamy, Joseph, 33
Botsford, Edmund, 9
Boyce, James P., 2, 4, 25–6, 31, 79–88
Brantly, W. T., 9, 13, 27, 99
Brewster, Paul, 30
Bullinger, Henrich, 43

Caldwell III, Robert W., 56
Calhoun, John C., 1
Calvin, John, 43
Calvinism, 2
　Baptist Edwardseanism, 17
　confessional, 3, 8, 17, 22, 90, 91, 102, 103
　dogmatic, 9
　eclectic populist, 17
　Edwardsean, 3
　evangelical, 102

five-point, 10, 22
Fullerite, 17
moderate, 8–39, 75, 95, 96, 102
Philadelphia Confession, 17
Campbell, McLeod, 75–78
Charleston Baptist Association, 83
Chun, Chris, 31
Confessions,
　Charleston, 2, 8, 16–22, 26, 42, 44, 47, 50, 67, 90, 91, 92, 103
　Philadelphia, 17–18
　Second London, 17–18, 23
　Westminster, 3
Cooley, Daniel W., 55, 78, 96, 103
Covenant Theology, 42–51
Crisp, Oliver, 4, 28, 55, 72, 73, 75–76, 78

Doddridge, Philip, 29
dueling, 36–37
Dwight, Timothy, 27–29

Edwards, Jonathan, 3, 10, 11, 25, 27, 28, 29, 30, 31, 34, 68, 74, 103
Edwards Jr., Jonathan, 72, 74, 95
Erickson, Millard, 99

Federalism, 1, 27
First Baptist Church of Charleston, 1, 17, 89, 102
Foster Jr., G. William, 4, 5, 8
Fuller, Andrew, 3, 15, 17, 26, 29–32, 84, 90, 102
Furman University, 4, 25, 38

Gano, John, 9, 63–64
Garrett, James Leo, 6, 100

Name/Subject Index

Gathercole, Simon, 4, 75, 77, 97
Gill, John, 102
Grotius, Hugo, 73, 74, 99

Hambrick-Stowe, Charles E., 27
Hamilton, Alexander, 19, 36, 37
Hamilton, S. Mark, 68
Hart, Oliver, 8, 14, 25, 40, 59, 69, 88, 98
Hartwell Sr., Jesse, 38
Haykin, Michael A. G., 14
Henry, Patrick, 7
Holifield, E. Brooks, 16, 17
Hopkins, Samuel, 28–29, 34, 93
honor, 7, 33–37, 60–62, 91
Horton, Michael, 100

imputation, 2, 29, 31, 32, 38–42, 54, 84, 90, 93, 96, 98

Jackson, Andrew, 1, 33
Johnson, William B., 2, 4, 5, 12, 24, 31, 58, 79–88, 90, 103
Judson, Adoniram, 26, 33
Judson, Ann Hasseltine, 33, 34
justice
   commutative, 2, 31–32, 94, 95
   distributive, 2, 31, 94, 95
   general, 94, 95
   rectoral, 2, 53, 68–70, 78, 86
   retributive, 2, 53, 68–70, 78
   satisfaction of, 31–32
justification, 40–42, 49, 52

Keach, Benjamin, 23

Mallary, Charles Dutton, 12–13
Manly Jr., Basil, 24
Manning, James, 16, 90
Maxcy, Jonathan, 15, 28, 54, 55, 90, 103
Mercer, Jesse, 12–13, 29, 55, 66
Methodism, 16, 25
Mims, James S., 12, 38
moral government, 2, 4, 14, 15, 24, 27–29, 30, 31, 33–34, 53–60, 68, 69, 71, 81–88, 93

Nettles, Thomas J., 1, 4–5, 6, 31, 42

New Divinity, 14, 15, 27–29, 33, 34, 56, 63, 67, 71, 72, 73, 84, 90, 92, 93, 94, 102
Noll, Mark, 27
non-penal substitution, 4, 72–79

Park, Edwards Amasa, 70, 93
Pearce, Samuel, 15, 29
penal non-substitution, 4, 72–79
penal substitution, 2, 4, 31, 41–42, 75, 95, 96, 99
Pendleton, James Madison, 66–67
Puritans, 43–44

reconciliation, 18–20
Reese, Joseph, 1
religious liberty, 1
Regular Baptists, 1
representation, 48, 62, 75
Reynolds, Alvin, 1, 6
Reynolds, James L., 12, 38
Richards, W. Wiley, 4, 8, 102
Rogers, James A., 6, 26
Roman Catholicism, 40

Screven, William, 17
slavery, 2, 33, 86
Smalley, John, 93
South Carolina Baptist Association, 1
Southern Baptist Theological Seminary, 25
Staughton, William, 15
Sweeney, Douglas A., 55, 78, 96, 103

Taylor, Nathaniel, 27–29
Triennial Convention, 10, 24, 25, 27, 102

unconditional election, 49

Waldo, John, 14
Washington, George, 17, 51
Whitefield, George, 25, 35
Wood, Gordon, 37
Wyatt-Brown, Betram, 33, 36

Yarnell III, Malcolm B., 92

Zwingli, Ulrich, 44

Scripture Index

OLD TESTAMENT

Exodus
14:30–31   57

Psalms
39:4   69
39:9   17
89:48   36, 70

NEW TESTAMENT

Romans
4   49
4:7–8   22
5   45–46, 97
8:34   23

Ephesians
5:2   23

Hebrews
2:17   23
7:25   23
8   50
9:28   23

1 Peter
2:24   23

www.ingramcontent.com/pod-product-compliance
Lightning Source LLC
Chambersburg PA
CBHW050839160426
43192CB00011B/2085